The Wealth *of* My Mother's Wisdom

THE
Wealth *of*
My Mother's
Wisdom

The Lessons That Made My Life Rich

TERRENCE JENKINS

*it*books

AN IMPRINT OF HARPERCOLLINS PUBLISHERS

itbooks

HarperCollins books may be purchased for educational, business, or sales promotional use. For information please e-mail the Special Markets Department at SPsales@harper collins.com.

A hardcover edition of this book was published in 2013 by It Books, an imprint of HarperCollins Publishers.

FIRST IT BOOKS PAPERBACK PUBLISHED 2014.

Designed by Renato Stanisic

Library of Congress Cataloging-in-Publication Data has been applied for.

ISBN 978-0-06-227295-9

14 15 16 17 18 ov/RRD 10 9 8 7 6 5 4 3 2 1

THIS BOOK IS DEDICATED TO LISA AND JAIME

Contents

Introduction

Thank you for picking up my book. I am very proud of it—though for a long time I wrestled with the very idea of writing a book at all. Sure, there are plenty of books out there by people who are my age, or even younger. Many of them have amazing stories of accomplishments to share, or have triumphed over terrible circumstances. I applaud those guys. But me, I feel like I am just getting started. What advice or guidance could I have to share? What about my stories makes them special? I haven't done enough yet, in my life, to write a memoir. I've been blessed with many amazing opportunities. I've worked hard, and played hard along the way. But a book? Give me a few more years and then we'll talk.

But the more I thought about it, the more I realized that the biggest gift I have in my life is the love and guidance of my family, and at the center of that, my mother. As I have learned after volunteering at the Boys & Girls Club over the years, there are many young men and women who have not had the benefit of a strong family unit the way I have. I feel my life, so far, has been led by a series of relatively good choices—first made by my mom when I was young, and then by me using the tools she gave me to guide my life. I knew that writing a book would allow me to share her wisdom with others—and to tell some of my own stories, showing how her guidance has always been the thing that I relied on most.

In these pages, you will meet a girl named Tiffany, who represents a few young ladies and men whom I have mentored throughout my years of volunteering. Certain identifying details have been changed to protect them. With Tiffany's story as the guide, I can pay it forward, as they say. Just as my mom relied on the examples her own mother set, I hope this book will inspire others to make good choices in their own lives.

I hope you will enjoy the stories in this book. For all the Tiffanys out there, I hope this book will give you some hope. For those of you who have followed my journey, thank you for supporting me, and I hope you find this book as entertaining to read as I found it to write.

And most of all, for my mom: Thanks for shaping me into the man I am.

The character of Tiffany is a composite based on girls I have mentored in recent years. All identifying details have been changed.

The Wealth *of* My Mother's Wisdom

Prologue

When my phone rang late one August night, my first reaction was to let it go to voice mail because I didn't recognize the number. I was jet-lagged, my neck was stiff, and my throat had that scratchy, about-to-get-sick feeling that inevitably sets in after a cross-country flight. I'd just landed in Los Angeles from New York and I had a long day of meetings and auditions ahead. It was 2:30 A.M. in L.A. (5:30 A.M. back home), an awkward time either way, and not usually a time associated with any good news. I needed to be on my A game, and the last thing I wanted was a distracting phone conversation. I really needed those last few hours of sleep, so of course I let the phone go to voice mail the first time. I was going to let it go to voice mail the second time, too, but when I went to hit "decline," my phone, which has a mind of its own, as always, answered the call instead.

To my surprise, the voice on the other end belonged to a teenage girl. I initially wanted to go into my broken Spanish accent and act like they had the wrong number. But after a few seconds, I realized who was calling: It was Tiffany.

I met Tiffany at the New York City chapter of the Boys & Girls Club of America. I'd been going up there once a month since I moved to New York City to host *106 & Park,* on BET. I went there to mentor kids in crisis. The idea of the Boys & Girls Club is pretty simple: They aim to provide kids in need with a safe place to hang out and consistent relationships with stable adults. The hope is that with this kind of support they can find both the positive outlook and the opportunities they need to make something of themselves. It's a great organization that's been helping kids for more than a hundred years. I was happy to be involved.

Tiffany had shown up at the Boys & Girls Club about six months earlier. She was seventeen years old, a smart, funny girl with an eye to her own future, but as is often the case, her family situation was not ideal. She was born in Atlanta, but her mom died when she was little, and her dad left a few years after that. As a preteen, she was sent to New York City to be raised by her grandmother. Her grandmother is super-religious, overprotective, and crazy strict, so of course they fought a lot—especially about Tiffany's boyfriend, Sean, a high school dropout with a juvenile rap sheet for petty theft. Usual story.

Tiffany was intellectually curious, and we initially connected over our mutual love of fashion. She would always comment on the outfits she saw me wear on *106 & Park*—letting me know if she approved or if my outfit was a "fail." She had no problem saying what she thought—and more times than not, she was right. She usually carried a black-and-gold laptop in her bag, and was always busy sketching, drawing, or looking at fashion blogs.

We shared a love of books, too. The first time she came to the center, I told Tiffany about my favorite of all time, *The Alchemist* by Paulo Coelho. She read it within a few days and came back, excited to tell me how much she liked it. We had a long, in-depth conversation about the journey of Santiago and chasing your own personal legend—your dream for your life. She told me about her own dream, of being a fashion designer, like her heroes Kimora Lee Simmons and Tracy Reese. She'd read an article about Daymond John, the businessman who started FUBU and took the fashion world by storm. She wanted to be like them, and I saw a lot of myself in her focus, ambition, and life goals.

But Tiffany was also her own worst enemy, smart but also too naive for her own good. She often hung out with the wrong crowd. She would earn good grades, and then sabotage herself by listening to bad advice from her party-mad friends. And she had a thing for bad boys, like Sean. Her behavior was the typical rebellious teen stuff, especially when you're living in a city like New York, and I could certainly relate, but it often seemed like she was having a hard time deciding who she truly wanted to be.

I'd been encouraging her to go to college, and she told me about her plan to apply to the Fashion Institute of Technology and a few other colleges that fall. So when I heard her voice on the phone that night, my first thought (after *How did she get my number?*) was that she needed some advice on her applications. But then I realized how late it was—this wasn't exactly the time of day to ask for college advice.

"Hi, Terrence? Yeah, hi—I'm kind of freaking out," I heard her say. "I had to talk to someone. I got your number from Dave, the adviser at the Boys and Girls Club . . ." She laughed, nervously. "It's not too late, is it?"

I groaned a little, reminding myself to kill Dave later for giving out my number to a seventeen-year-old girl. But if Tiffany was persistent enough to get my digits, there must be a reason she needed to talk to me. I knew I should hear her out.

I rolled over, glanced at the clock. For me, mentoring usually began and ended when I walked through the door of the Boys & Girls Club. I love the organization with all my heart, but I'm no one's parent, and I'm *especially* no one's parent at 2:30 in the morning. I thought about asking Tiffany to call back tomorrow, but something in her voice made me hesitate. So maybe I'd have bags

4

under my eyes during the meeting the next day. She was clearly upset about something.

"Nope, it's fine. What's up?"

"I'm pregnant," she blurted out. "And I need . . . I don't know . . . advice?"

I went silent. I don't even remember what my initial response was—some platitudes along the lines of *Wow, how tough, I'm sorry to hear that*. I honestly didn't know how to react: I'm at the age where my college friends are settling down and getting married, so when someone tells me they are pregnant it's usually great news. But I could tell that Tiffany was shaken up. What could I say to calm her down?

Inside I was thinking, *Why me? I can't offer her good advice. I'm just a never-married single guy. I know nothing about what it's like to be a pregnant teenage girl. I'm just happy the girl I'm dating isn't calling me and saying she's pregnant. The last thing I want to do is have this conversation. Besides, I really need to be fresh for my meeting tomorrow.*

By now, Tiffany was crying for real. I felt myself growing frantic: "Have you tried to talk to a teacher, or someone at the center?"

She mumbled something about how she wanted to talk to someone who really *understood* her.

"Look," I told her, "I can't talk now, but we'll meet when I get back to New York and will figure something out then. Okay?" We agreed to meet up at the center later that week. I figured that by that point I'd have a whole notebook of numbers of counselors who were better equipped to help her than I was.

But that night, I wasn't able to sleep. I kept thinking about Tiffany's voice, how emotional she was, how vulnerable and raw. I felt like I'd let her down. Finally, growing frustrated, I turned on the light and began paging through the *Think Like a Man* script, which I was studying in preparation for my upcoming role. And that's when it hit me.

I love my mom to death, and we have a really great relationship. But I'm not a mama's boy, not to any extent. In fact, I hadn't really known that much about my mom's past until I got the role of Michael in *Think Like a Man*—a man who *is* a mama's boy. As preparation for the role, I'd spent the last few months "researching" my mom: talking to her about her childhood, getting to know her better, and spending more time with her, one on one, then I ever had. Our relationship had really evolved during these talks, as I'd come to fully appreciate the decisions she'd made in raising me. For the first time, I had real clarity about the inspirational role she'd played in my life.

As I lay there considering Tiffany's circumstances, I remembered something my mom always says: Nothing happens by coincidence. God is always sending us opportunities to help other people. Yes, I was probably the worst person to give advice about parenting and raising a kid: I have no kids, not even a dog. I may have a huge amount of responsibility at work and to my coworkers, but I still have a lot to learn when it comes to relationships. So I'm the last person to offer any advice about the right time for motherhood. But after spending these last couple of months with my mom and learning so much about the challenges she had faced raising me, I realized I did have one thing to offer Tiffany: my mom's stories, and my own.

Back when my mom was seventeen, she was faced with the same dilemma: pregnant, unmarried, still in high school. A lot of girls in her situation would have walked away—abortion, adoption, abandonment, you name it. But my mom worked it out, made some tough choices, and gave birth to me. It's fair to say that everything I have become, all my achievements, I owe to the lessons that I learned from her. She was strong, independent-minded, and courageous from the jump.

I found myself thinking of the child that Tiffany might give birth to in nine months' time and the impact that she could potentially have on that kid's life. People talk a lot about the importance of the dynamic between fathers and sons, or mothers and daughters; but what about the connection between mothers and their sons? A great relationship with his mom can change everything for a man. It did for me.

It's amazing how much my mom did in her life, on my behalf.

Even though, as a seventeen-year-old single mom with relatively little help, all the chips were stacked against her, she was able to provide an incredible amount of support for me. I've had some amazing opportunities, from being the first in my family to graduate from college, to starring in movies that grossed more than $100 million worldwide; from being a young African American male on television every day as a host, to interviewing President Obama—and all of them are due very much in part to the work ethic my mom instilled in me. Because of her belief in me, because of her careful grooming, I had been blessed with a very rich life, full of both financial and personal success that I could hardly believe. But even more important than the money was the way Mom's lessons enriched my spirit, my emotions, and my relationship with God.

Maybe sharing my mom's stories with Tiffany would help her through her crisis, even offer her some encouragement about motherhood. No, I didn't have specific parenting advice to offer, but I could certainly provide a shoulder to cry on. And considering that, in *Think Like a Man*, I was set to play a character dating a single mother raising a young boy, it also felt like an omen.

These are the stories Tiffany and I shared over the following months. My hope was that my mom's stories would inspire not just Tiffany, but other people as well—in the same way that my mom inspired and shaped me.

1

My Mother's Words of Wisdom
About Courage & Sacrifice

*W*e met at the Boys & Girls Club last night. I got there ten *minutes early, but Tiffany was already waiting for me in the lobby, wearing her usual stylish outfit. When she spied me coming through the door, she jumped up and ran over and started talking my ear off. At first, I was tentative about what to say—was she still trying to decide whether or not to have the baby? While I'm certainly glad my mom chose to have me, abortion is a personal decision and I didn't want to be asked my opinion about that. But I quickly figured out from the way Tiffany was talking about "this baby" that she had already decided to go ahead with the pregnancy.*

In fact, she soon began to tell me about the storybook life she was envisioning for her future. "I figure, I'll go to college and learn fashion design while Sean gets a job and supports us, and maybe my grandma will watch the baby while I'm studying. And then when the kid's old

*enough to start school I can start my own clothing company or open a
store or something. That doesn't sound so bad, does it?" She looked at
me for affirmation.*

*"Not at all," I said, though I wasn't sure how realistic it was. "Is
Sean on board?"*

*Sean knew about the pregnancy, she said. At first he had freaked out
a little bit ("Scratch that—more like, a lot"), but he had offered to step
up to the plate. "I mean, he's not exactly a contributing member of society at the moment," she said, laughing, but only a little. "But he's pretty
smart, believe it or not. He says he'll get a job. And his mom is actually
really excited to be a grandma."*

"That's great."

*"It is. It's gonna be great." And then, out of the blue, she was cry-
ing. When she calmed down a little, she wiped her nose on the sleeve
of her shirt and said, "You must think I'm a total fool. A pregnant
teenage girl—what a cliché. Like an episode of 16 and Pregnant or
something."*

*"You're not the first teenage girl this has happened to. You're not
even the first teenage girl I've known that has been in this situation."*

"Honestly?" she whispered. "I'm scared shitless."

*And that seemed as good a time as any to start telling her about my
mother.*

. . . . .

MY MOM, LISA, WAS seventeen years old when she found out she was pregnant with me. It was the early eighties, in Jamaica, Queens, New York City, and the beginning of one of the worst periods in the city's history. New York was totally different then from what it's like today. Broadway and 42nd Street were wall-to-wall peep shows. People were struggling financially; homelessness was becoming a real problem; and racial tension was high. Homicide rates were already three times higher than they are today, and they hadn't even peaked yet.

And then there were the drugs. Jamaica, Queens, had it as bad if not worse than any other neighborhood. By 1982, the crack epidemic was in full swing. Nancy Reagan was telling America to Just Say No, but in Jamaica, Queens, the epicenter of the epidemic, most everyone was saying yes. Here, the drug dealers were king: Kenneth "Supreme" McGriff and his nephew, Gerald "Prince" Miller; Lorenzo "Fat Cat" Nichols and Howard "Pappy" Mason. The "Supreme Team" gang headquartered their drug operations (which, at its peak, sold $250,000 of crack a day) out of the Baisley Park housing project, not far from where my mom grew up with her mother Helen, brother Clarence, and her grandma Nana.

Where Mom lived during high school wasn't so bad—her neighborhood was mostly families living in small houses racked up next to each other—but the area surrounding her apartment was getting worse by the day. Gangs were slowly taking over the streets.

In some areas you could get shot just walking down to the corner store. Graffiti covered the subways, the buildings. Derelict buildings were being used as crack dens and whorehouses. Crime was so bad that people would post signs in their cars saying "No Radio," in hopes that crack addicts wouldn't break the car windows yet again, looking for anything they could turn into drug money.

It was a tough neighborhood to live in, to say the least, but my mom was doing her best. In bad times, she was a good girl—raised Baptist, a good student, a Girl Scout. Her divorced mom struggled to support the family working as a dietician at hospitals—at times, my mom and her siblings shared a bed, because money was too tight and their apartment was too small for separate bedrooms—but my grandma kept tight reins on my mom. She was a latchkey kid, but my grandma had her on a strict schedule of church, chores, and school: When my mom wasn't studying, she was usually cooking meals or shoveling snow or wheeling the laundry down to the local Laundromat. She didn't go spend the night at friends' houses. She wasn't even allowed to visit girlfriends if my grandma knew there would be brothers hanging around. She was very sheltered, and very protected.

At school, Mom was popular, charismatic, and athletic—she took dance classes and ran on the track team. At her high school, Springfield High, there were constant gang fights, even kids getting killed, but she kept her head down and focused. It was her last year of high school, and she was planning to be the first person in her family to graduate from college. She was set to attend Hunter in the fall.

Then she fell in love. My biological father was the first man she'd ever seriously dated. The fact that he was nearly ten years older than she was made her think he was mature, a real man, regardless of the fact that he was a small-time drug dealer. Within the year, she was pregnant.

Maybe another girl would have taken a different route—a lot of girls her age got abortions—and there were definitely people in her life who told her, "You don't have to go through with this." But my mom was raised religious, and despite her guilt about her situation, it was never a debate for her whether or not she was going to have me. She was going to be a mother.

And that's when her boyfriend showed his true colors, and bailed out on her.

My mom had had very limited contact with his family—and clearly, they didn't want to support a child. And the bigger my mom got, the less *he* was around, too. Finally, he was a no-show for my birth.

She was really frightened. As she told me, "All of a sudden, it was, 'This is the person I got involved with? My first love? Unfortunately, he is a man-child. He was clearly not responsible enough to take care of his responsibilities.' " And that was it for Mom. She decided that if he wasn't going to step up to the plate to help her when I was born, then she needed to move on and totally cut him out of her life—and mine. She wasn't going to sue him for child support, wasn't going to try to get him to do his share of the parenting, wasn't going to waste a second thinking about him. It would be as if he never existed at all.

This was an instrumental decision for my mom; a decision that, before I was old enough to understand it, would have a big influence on who I would become as a man. I've witnessed, over the years, how people in relationships sometimes hold on and fight for people or things that aren't worth fighting for. But what my mom's decision taught me later in life was that if a person lets you know who they really are, through their actions, believe them.

My mom's situation was unique, of course—I'm not saying it's always a good idea to cut a father out of a kid's life, or that child support isn't important. Raising a child on your own—I can only imagine—is one of the hardest things in the world to do. But in this particular circumstance, my mom looked at the situation and asked herself, "What's the better use of my time and energy? Chasing down a man who doesn't want to be here? Trying to fix a person who doesn't want to be fixed? Trying to make him a more mature person, so he can be a father to my son?" She realized that trying to continue the relationship with my biological father would be like raising two children. Having him involved in her son's upbringing, even financially, would only hinder her growth and mine.

The courageous decision that my mom made to just move on gave her freedom and independence. Instead of fighting with my biological father and spending her energy going to court, throwing bricks through his window, or cursing him out for not doing what she wanted him to do, she shifted her energy in a more positive direction. She turned her focus on to me, and her own personal progress.

Knowing that my mom had made this decision gave me all kinds of perspective on my own life. Sometimes you just hit a dead end—with a relationship, a job, a friendship, a career path. And if you feel like the situation isn't making you a better person, isn't making you stronger, isn't leading you down the path that would make your heart and God happy, why fight it? You're swimming against the current. And sometimes you just have to look down at things from a bird's-eye view to see what's best for you. It's better to let go of what you know isn't working and find a healthier path.

My mom had a very strong sense of independence, which is one of the traits that I'm most happy to have inherited from her. Over the course of your lifetime, people come and go: friendships, relationships, coworkers, even people you trust. You meet people that help and inspire you, and others that let you down and betray you. But no matter whom my mom encountered, she never let the actions of other people dictate her life or take her off her path. And from the day I was born, Mom never allowed anyone into her circle who might take her away from the task at hand: me.

This is what she told me about the day she met me:

> When I had you, the first thing I remember is that we locked eyes. And I knew I belonged to you and you belonged to me. I saw that you had green eyes and beautiful skin, and jet-black hair. Then I opened up the blanket and made sure you had all your fingers and toes. Once I had that assurance, I breathed a sigh of relief and thought, It's all good.

At this, Tiffany began to get teary again. But it seemed like a good kind of teary—and I could see that she was excited about the idea of having a little pal of her own. She got a faraway, dreamy look on her face, as if she was imagining the fantasy life that my mom and I must have lived, the one that she might be able to live, too. "So how did she work out the whole college thing with a baby?" she asked.

Unfortunately, she didn't. The hard truth is that my birth changed all of Mom's plans. She'd already started her liberal arts degree at Hunter College when I was born, but it very quickly became clear that raising a child on her own while going to school wasn't going to work. These were the days before online classes, the Internet, and a lot of the tools that are available today. So she dropped out of college, went on public assistance, and stayed home with me until I could talk. (As she told me, "I wanted you to be able to tell me what was going on, if something happened at day care." Mom was always very protective, and practical!)

For a while, we lived with my grandma, but by the time Mom was nineteen and I was one, we were living on our own. She got a job working at the World Trade Center as a secretary/receptionist.

Life for us back then was really stripped down. She woke up and went to work, then came straight home and took care of me. That's the full extent of it. We had one television in the house, and a record player, where she played Michael Jackson, Whitney Houston, Stevie Wonder, and Marvin Gaye tracks, all those great hits of the seventies and eighties. Outside of her job, Mom was 100 percent focused on me. Weekends were about taking me to the park, or the zoo, or riding a train to the beach—just the two of us.

In a way, it was a simpler time to be a single mom—there weren't so many distractions that could take you away from your kid in the eighties. I work with young parents all the time at the Boys & Girls Club, and I see that they are constantly on their phones or laptops, checking Instagram and Mobli and Twitter and Facebook. They're going to nightclubs, going on trips—there are just so many things to do that are tempting, that distract you from the often-difficult grind of raising a kid. That's surely got to be a challenge for any teen mom today, but in my mom's day, life wasn't as crowded with all of these kinds of distractions.

But that doesn't mean it was easy. I can't imagine what those first few years were like for her, having missed her chance to experience the world, attend college, and have adult relationships. Now, she was all alone with a baby. There she was, a black teenager in drug-ravaged Queens, not even old enough to vote, and trying to figure out how to raise a kid all by herself.

I admire my mother so much for the choices she made during this time in our lives. I think back to when *I* was seventeen: I was still incredibly wild and reckless. Even now, at age thirty, I don't know if I have the maturity to raise a baby. My best friend just had a beautiful daughter, and I'm still terrified to hold her because I don't want to break her! The idea of being in charge of another human being's life? It scares me to death. Having a child requires not just responsibility and patience, it also requires a tremendous amount of courage, no matter *how* old you are, but especially when you're that young.

But here's the thing. My mom's courage had a really profound effect on me. You've got to have courage if you're going to take any risks in life—it's something that lets you expand beyond the box that you're born in to, to really grow as a person. And my mom taught me by example; she showed some serious bravery from the start. My mom tells me that, from day one of having me, she kept telling herself, *I can do this: I can raise a son and be successful at doing it*, and that mind-set carried her through all the challenges to come. I am incredibly grateful.

Being in a creative industry—like acting, or being a fashion designer—means that you are constantly putting yourself and your work out in front of people to be judged, and you have to be courageous every day. Every time I walk into an audition to face a panel of agents, directors, and managers—everyone looking at me, waiting for me to make a mistake—I'm putting myself on the line. If I were to go into these situations without confidence, I'd never get hired. I'd never be successful. But I inherited my mother's mind-set of *I can do this; nothing is going to stop me.* Her courage stands as a constant inspiration. If she could raise a newborn into a man—and there's nothing harder than that—then there is nothing holding me back from going for all the things I want in life, no matter how difficult they seem. When I walk into that room, I am never afraid, thanks to her.

We fell silent for a little bit. Tiffany fiddled with the hem of her skirt, running her fingers along the stitches. "Sounds like your mom had it tough. It's hard to imagine you ever being on welfare," she said. "But your mom gave birth to you way back in the day, right? I'm kidding, but seriously, times have changed. I bet it's easier now for a single mom to have it all. You can have a kid and go to college and have a job and go out partying with your girlfriends on the weekends. Right?" Tiffany looked at me, seeking reassurance.

Growing up, my mom always told me that when you decide to have a baby, you have to come to terms with the fact that your life isn't just your own anymore. You have to make sure that *someone else* is healthy, protected, and safe. It's a sacrifice, and one of the reasons my mom was so dedicated to raising me right was that she understood that sacrifice and was fully committed to it. She understood her own priorities. Sometimes that selfishness that we all have as teens—selfishness that is completely normal, and that I have suffered from myself—has to be jettisoned for the greater good of your child.

When you're a parent, every decision you make—the friends you hang with, the people you date, the job and the hours you take on, the choice to drink or smoke or hang out late or surround yourself with violence, the movies that you watch around your kids, the music you listen to—creates the world that shapes your child. My mom's number one priority was protecting me, always, no matter how hard the decision was. For her the question was always, "Is this a good environment for my child? Is this a good person to have hanging around my child?" It didn't matter if it was a friend, her mom, or her brother; I always, always came first.

I look back and I realize how hard my mom was always working on my behalf. Those first few years we were inseparable. She would literally strap me to her back and take me everywhere she went. To the beach, to the Laundromat, to the grocery store, to the park, just to do errands: Whatever she had to do, I was always with her. Part of this was out of necessity—she couldn't afford and didn't trust babysitters—but part of it was her desire to expose me to the world. She wanted me to experience everything. As I grew up, she gave me swimming lessons, enrolled me in after-school programs, encouraged me to try sports, showed me as much of New York City as she could. Instead of letting me play video games or watch movies while she relaxed, she constantly read books to me. The things she'd never had growing up? She gave them to me when she could. The things she missed out on in her own life? She gladly gave them up so I could have more. Maybe I wasn't headed to private school, or mastering the piano at a young age, but considering that I was growing up in one of the most dangerous cities in the country at the time, Mom really created the best environment for me that she could.

It's not like my mom was some kind of saint. But she sacrificed a lot for me. I didn't understand that at the time—I wouldn't until much, much later—but I certainly saw her prioritizing my needs ahead of hers. And that taught me a critical lesson about the importance of putting others before yourself. Sure, my mom's sacrifice give me the stability and the security that I needed to thrive, the safety to explore and grow, but it also demonstrated for me how love is about giving, not selfishness. That understanding helped me grow as a man, and has definitely improved my relationships with friends and girlfriends.

Here's the thing about sacrifice: When you do it right, the person you're doing it for should never know what you gave up for him.

Let me tell you a story. I once talked to Ryan Seacrest about hosting, and asked him for some advice. He shared with me the advice that Dick Clark had given *him*. He told me, "People should be able to look at you hosting and think that they can do it, too. They should watch what you're doing and think it looks *easy*; that they could just walk off the street and step into your job. That's how you know you're a good host. Because it's a lot harder than people think. You're balancing what people are saying in your earpiece, looking at scripts, interviewing talent, dealing with the crowd, connecting with the audience, holding your mic, looking at the camera, articulating your speech. It's a very complicated art form. But if you're a good host, no one will have any idea that any of that is going on behind the scenes."

I think that lesson is very applicable to being a good parent. My mom made raising me look easy. I never looked at her and thought that she was struggling, or that raising me was complicated or challenging for her. She did a good job of shielding me from the difficult emotional side of what she had to do, from the challenges that she was facing every day.

I'm sure my mother had some really tough times. But she never had any breakdowns in front of me. She never made me feel like I was a burden in her life. I never understood until later how much she was doing for my sake. Because of that, I grew up with a real sense of security. Security and stability, along with love, are the best gifts you can give a child.

In Her Own Words: Terrence's Mom, Lisa, on Parenting & Sacrifice

If you love your children, you sacrifice for them. As a mom, this was how I lived my life. I may have needed braces, but I didn't get them until I was in my forties—I made sure Terrence got the braces he needed first, so he could present his smile. I never splurged on clothes or shoes because I wanted to make sure Terrence had supplies for school. It was more important to make sure Terrence had the books he needed.

I believe we're at a stage where there's a lot of selfishness going on in our society. Parents are not there for their children. And "being there" isn't always about providing material things, either—it's about being present for the everyday grind. Your children need you there for those days when they come home and have homework that they can't figure out. There might be that bully in the school that they want to figure out how to handle, or a parent-teacher conference they want you to attend.

If we are selfish, and unwilling to sacrifice our time and our own desires, our society is going to end up with a lot of broken youth. Young men, especially, are distracted these days—with social media, with Facebook, their lives are disjointed. They are distracted, and our kids are suffering. Kids are crying out for our help, now, and it's our duty and responsibility to be there for them. Not once a month, but every day. As parents we have to be present. You can't divide your attention. Your kids need you to be there, to watch them, to see who their friends are. If you aren't, you miss a lot of moments, and sometimes signs of larger issues.

My mom is in a nursing home now. And I never forget all the sacrifices she made for me. My mom is old school—she never asked for anything. But I know how much she protected me growing up. My mom was always on the case, looking out for me, making sure I had the basics. I turned into a strong woman because of her. So now, there's nothing I wouldn't get for her. I buy her everything I can afford: I like to say, "What baby wants, baby gets."

Sacrifice is about making sure the people you love have what they need to succeed in life, even if you have to go without. Because when they succeed, you succeed. And when they win, you win.

Kevin Liles Talks About His Mom

Kevin Liles is the former president of Def Jam Recordings and executive vice president of the Warner Music Group. An entrepreneur and author, in 2009, Kevin launched his own company, KWL Management, where he has overseen the careers of many stars, including Trey Songz, Nelly, and Big Sean. He's a mentor and friend, and I am honored he shared this story about his mother with me.

My mom was seventeen years old when she had me. I don't think she had any idea what a mom should be, but she had every idea that she wanted my life to be better than hers. When you have a woman who wants to sacrifice herself so you can have a better life, what better mom could there be?

My biological father fought in Vietnam, came home, and struggled with drugs. My stepfather, whom I call my father, came into our lives when I was two years old. We had one great family. My grandparents took care of us while my parents worked. So growing up, we had love, we had food, we had family; we didn't have a lot of money, but we experienced a lot of great things.

My mom was the influence for my career. She always felt like people limit themselves because of their lack of experience. So she taught me to be not a product of my environment, but a product of my experiences. Meet new people, travel to new places, do new things, have new friends. She never let me limit myself: I went to school, I played sports my whole life, I had a scholarship for engineering, and I ended up becoming the president of Def Jam. You can't write that story. If it weren't for her I wouldn't be where I am today.

My mom was willing to sacrifice herself. Often, she wasn't home: she worked two jobs every day, went to school, and took on a senior position at her job in order to fund the things she gave to my brother and me. When I was young, I called my grandmother and grandfather "Mom" and "Dad"—they were retired, and they were the ones caring for us every day while my parents were out there working to provide a better life for us. I didn't give my parents the respect of calling them Mom and Dad: I called them by their first names.

I remember my mom saying, "If you keep calling us Alberta and Jerome, we're going to punish you." And I got it quickly. I had to write "Mom and Dad" five hundred times every time I called them by their first names. I still have those papers!

My mom was also a dreamer. One of the things she always said was, "I believe in myself, therefore I am what I believe myself to be." That sat with me. What I realize now, every day, is that God gave us gifts and we have to use those gifts to make a difference in the world.

2

My Mother's Words of Wisdom
About Love & Acceptance

*I*t's a boy.

   Tiffany was practically bouncing with excitement when we met up last night. She'd gone in for an ultrasound that morning and learned the gender of her baby. In five months time she's going to have a son, a little boy of her own.

   I'd found Tiffany sitting on the sidelines of the gym at the Boys & Girls Club, busy sketching outfits in that design notebook she always carried in her bag. She was oblivious to the basketball game taking place just feet away. Being pregnant hadn't eliminated her fashion sense— she was still dolled up, though underneath her leggings and tunic you could definitely see a real baby bump. She spent most of the time we were together with her hand placed on top of her stomach, as if she were trying to reach through and touch the baby boy who was growing inside her.

"My little man," she said, and smiled. "It's like he's already talking to me!"

At home, though, things weren't exactly playing out as she'd hoped. She seemed more worried, as if the reality of her situation was starting to hit home. Her super-religious grandmother was less than happy about the out-of-wedlock pregnancy, and although she hadn't kicked Tiffany off the sleeper sofa, she wasn't offering to help out, either. Tiffany was trying to save up for the baby, so she got a job after school as a waitress at a coffee shop. But being on her feet all evening was already getting hard; she was worried about how she'd manage when she was eight months pregnant. And although she fired off applications to four different colleges, she'd just found out how much tuition costs at some of her top choices, and nearly had a heart attack.

And then there was Sean. She wasn't sure what to think about him. First he told her that he was on board 100 percent, and that he was going to provide for them both—Tiffany and the baby. But as far as Tiffany could tell, he hadn't applied for a single job. He was staying out late, drinking with his buddies and hitting up the clubs, while she worked late shifts at the restaurant. While she used to feel they were "totally connected" all the time, now she was worried when she saw him "liking" Instagram photos of other women, or following cute girls she didn't know on Twitter.

"He used to call me every day, and now he's just sending me text messages filled with emoticons," Tiffany said, frustrated. "I mean,

it's not like he's doing anything wrong, not that I can point to—his Facebook status still says he's in a relationship with me—but it pisses me off."

Man, I really felt for her. I've certainly been guilty of relying on IMs instead of real communication; these days, with all the social media that is available, it is pretty confusing knowing how to behave in a relationship, let alone while being pregnant. I truly hoped that Sean would man up soon—he's a good kid, I think, just a little confused about what it means to be responsible, and at that age who isn't?

But to make Tiffany feel better right now, I decided to tell her about my mom and her own journey toward love.

I'VE NEVER MET MY biological father—in fact, I don't know anything about him, beyond his name. I don't know because I've never asked, even though my mom offered to tell me anything I wanted to know. But see, I've never *wanted* to know. And the reason I don't want to know is because I already have a dad. My *real* dad, Jaime Gonzalez. He married my mom and adopted me when I was three years old, and I've never met a better man.

Here's the thing about Jaime. He's a light-skinned, six-foot-one, 360-pound second-generation Puerto Rican New Yorker—a Nuyorican, as they like to say. He talks with a thick New Yawk accent. He's witty and opinionated: He holds strong views about everything from religion to politics to work, and he doesn't bite his tongue. We used to frequently butt heads.

And my mom? She's barely five feet one, a tiny beautiful slip of a thing, with rich chocolate skin and long black hair and a snappy wardrobe. She's got a New York edge but also a big dollop of that southern hospitality, with just a hint of a southern drawl in her voice. She's politically correct, and although she's outgoing, she's very careful with what she says. Sure, she'll tell you off—in a polite way—but then she'll say, "Have a nice day," and you'll still be cool the next day.

They are a study in juxtaposition.

So no, Jaime isn't exactly the person that my mom imagined herself ending up with, back when she was in high school. Never in a million years did she think that she would date someone who wasn't African American. It just wasn't in her consciousness. But the story of how Jaime courted her is a real lesson in what love really can—and should—be.

I was already two years old, and my mom still hadn't started dating again. She was so torn up by her experience with my biological father that, frankly, she wasn't very interested in giving love another go. Besides, her focus was me, 100 percent, and raising a toddler doesn't, or shouldn't, leave much time for meeting potential suitors.

But one day, when she was working the front desk of a company called Atwood Richards in the World Trade Center, Jaime walked in the door. He'd come to fix the card access security system for the building, but what really stuck with him that day was my mother. As he tells it, she immediately impressed him—by both her beauty and her "good aura."

My mom was gun shy in the beginning, and they had some false starts: Jaime would ask her out, and she would agree to meet him at the front door after work, but then she would have second thoughts and sneak out the back instead. "I must have missed you in the lobby," she'd tell him. What she was *really* thinking was: "If he's a real man, he'll pursue me." And he did. He was crazy persistent—he just wouldn't quit. Finally, he seduced her with sugar—he left a box of gourmet cookies on her desk. Those cookies were so good that she agreed to go out with him—but just to find out where he bought them. After work that day, he escorted her to David's Cookies, down on Wall Street. (It's still there to this day, and makes a mean chocolate chip cookie.)

During that walk, Jamie asked my mom about her goals in life. My mom was totally floored by that question: No one had ever asked before. She thought about this for a long time and then finally told him three things. She wanted me to graduate from college, since she hadn't. She wanted to own a dog—because pets are symbolic of home, stability, and all the important learned life skills and responsibilities. And she wanted to own a house. Outright. This was something her own mom had never been able to do.

Jaime listened carefully and said, "I can do those things for you."

That was the moment when my mom knew that he was the one for her, but she still put him through the ringer—for my sake. One of the first things she told him, during that walk to the bakery, was all about me. "I have a son," she said, right off the bat—because she was a package deal now, and if he wasn't mature enough to deal with that, she wanted to know it before she wasted any more time with him. But it didn't deter him a bit. He just said, "Okay," and kept on walking.

Their first real date—like almost all of their early dates—was spent at our home. When he arrived at the door, he was carrying a box of Pampers diapers. I answered the door because my mom was in the bathroom getting ready. I looked at my future stepfather and said, "Mama's in the toilet making doodoo." (Disclaimer: She wasn't!) I don't think she's ever forgiven me for that.

That didn't scare him away, either. Instead, he began wooing my mother by befriending me. He would show up for dates with jugs of apple juice—my favorite—and pound cakes, and endless boxes of diapers. He spent hours reading me my favorite Sweet Pickles book, over and over: *Goose Goofs Off.* This floored my mom—"This is a real man," she thought. Jaime and I had great chemistry from the start. The first time we met, I jumped on him and tried to wrestle with him. I would chant his name over and over—"Jaime Jaime Jaime."

Still, my mom made Jaime work for her love. She wanted to test him to make sure he was going to be a responsible, loving, caring person—not just for her sake, but also for mine. She wouldn't even kiss him for months—you would have thought they were back in the Victorian age. Instead, they spent all their time with me, playing board games and checkers and cards in my grandmother's backyard. When they weren't together, he even wrote her love letters and sent her poetry.

Within a year, they were engaged. They ended up getting married twice. The first time was for my benefit: My mom wanted to move in with Jaime, because his neighborhood had a better pediatrician and day care. But her family disapproved of them living together before marriage. So they hit up the courthouse and got married right away so they could put me in the Little Friends preschool. Four months later, they had a "proper" wedding. And they've been married ever since—twenty-seven years.

The moral of this story, at least I think so, is that you never have to settle—there's going to be someone out there for you, even if they aren't what you think you're looking for. As my mom knew, a *real* man will fight to be with a woman if he loves her; he's even willing to struggle if that's what it means. He won't just be around for the easy times. If he wants you at your best, he will have to love you at your worst. That's a lesson I absorbed from watching how Jaime adored and cared for my mother.

Something my mom says is that if a person is not present, they aren't supposed to be part of your destiny. My biological father wasn't there, but Jaime was. And my mom chose him for both of us.

As a young man, growing up with my stepdad, I did sometimes have questions about the biological father whom I'd never met. But as I grew and matured, I realized what a great stepdad I had in my life. I came to understand that living without the distraction of a "dad" who didn't want to be around had allowed me to focus on someone who *wanted* to be a real father. It showed me that my mom had really made the right decision.

My mom tells me that she once asked her mom, "In all your years on this earth, what is the most important thing you learned?" She expected her to say something profound or religious.

Instead, my grandma replied, "Don't be worried about any man who ain't worried about you." Clearly, it's a lesson that all the women in my mom's family have taken to heart.

So as far as Tiffany and Sean went, I wasn't going to offer specific relationship advice—God knows I'm not perfect at relationships, either. And of course it's important for a kid to have his father in his life. But if a man wants to be around, he'll be around. And if he doesn't, it's time to look for someone else.

Tiffany didn't look very happy to hear this. "Yeah, but look at me"—she gestured to her baby bump. "I'm huge." I rolled my eyes at this, but she went on. "Anyway, it's not like guys are gonna be beating down my door when I'm carrying a kid around all day. Maybe I should just focus on fixing what I've got."

That's not necessarily true. In fact, my mom always said that being a single mom was an opportunity, not a disadvantage, when it came to dating. That might sound strange, but hear me out. Mom always said that if you already have a child, you get to actively choose the man who is going to be that kid's father, and *decide* who is going to raise him. It's not just the default job of the guy who happened to knock you up—especially if that guy isn't showing much interest in being a dad. When you are dating with a kid, you get to see how the men you go out with behave around children, what they are really like when it comes to those kinds of adult decisions. And as my mom likes to say, that's a really powerful position to be in. Anyone can father a kid, but a real man will be a *father.*

Jamie is one of the best men I've ever met—he was willing and eager to take on two people, instead of just one. And that's how you know it's for real. If someone really loves a woman, they will love her child as well. It's not just about attraction or sex; it's about loving someone so much you *want* to bring their kid diapers and read *Goose Goofs Off* a hundred times. This shows that someone's game to be there for the everyday grind—the fevers and the potty training and the visits to the emergency room at three A.M. That's the kind of person *all* women should be with—not just single moms. But single moms get the opportunity to give a partner a test drive, so to speak, to see how they act under pressure, before committing to them.

Jaime was the game changer for my mom and me. He became the foundation of our lives. He brought us the stability that we needed in order to thrive. Those goals my mom had? He helped her achieve every single one, before she was thirty-five.

Tiffany digested this quietly, picking at her fingernails—bright pink, manicured. The girl was still thinking about her appearance. Finally, she changed the subject. "Was it really that big a deal back then that your dad was Puerto Rican? I mean, half my friends are in interracial relationships."

It was definitely progressive back then for a black woman to be married to a fair-skinned Puerto Rican. (Puerto Ricans come in all colors, from white to caramel to jet black; Jaime is Spanish speaking but looks like a white Italian.) This was way before *Jungle Fever.* The world has changed a lot since the 1980s, but at the time, they were still an anomaly.

At one point, my mom asked Jaime if he was worried about being in an interracial relationship. His answer was "I don't see you as a black woman—I just see you as a beautiful woman. Your color is like body paint to me." With that answer, he made her feel very special about being a chocolate-colored African American woman—at a time when there weren't a lot of positive images of this. And she realized that if he was okay walking around the streets with a black woman on his arm, then she would be okay with a "white" man on hers.

As she put it to me recently, "You never know what color a gift is going to be. And your father was a gift. You shouldn't turn away a gift just because you aren't sure about the color of the wrapping paper it arrived in. Anyway, in life, most people only see green: If you can't pay your bills, they don't care what color you are."

That's not to say that they didn't run up against prejudice. Mom's family initially opposed the match, and one of Jaime's best friends told him that he shouldn't marry a black woman. They persevered anyway. When our family moved to North Carolina in the early nineties, this was a whole new world. We had a tough time trying to find a church. The churches in North Carolina were segregated: There were churches for white people, and black people, and not a lot of mixing. People that my parents encountered in that part of the world were sometimes petty and judgmental—people would come right up to my mom and rudely ask her why she was married to a white man. It made my mom very uncomfortable.

I have a lot of respect for my mom for being able to see that it's the person inside that matters, not their ethnic background or the way they look. And her choice taught me never, ever to judge people for who they choose to be with. I am a straight man and I love my black women, but I have no problem with gay marriage; I have no problem with interracial relationships. Black, white—whatever floats your boat, love can transcend skin color and ethnic background and even gender.

And not only did their marriage teach me never to judge other people's relationship choices, it left me a lot more open about people in general. I grew up surrounded by people of all ethnicities—not just white and black, but Italian and Indian and Spanish. I was taught that the only thing that mattered was character. What's important is who you are, what you do, what kind of person you want to be. Are you a family person? Do you care about your community? Do you take pride in your work? Do you take responsibility for your actions? That's what's important—not skin color. That's a powerful thing to learn at a young age.

This has also helped me a lot in my career. When I sit down for an interview with someone, I don't see any skin color, and I don't judge them in advance.

Tiffany nodded. I could see I was getting somewhere.

Sure. But even more important than lessons about skin color were the lessons that my parent's relationship has taught me about respect. I learned from watching them together that men should treat women like *ladies*. I saw that played out every day at home. From the first day they met, Jaime behaved like a real gentleman—it takes a special kind of guy to court a woman for months without even a kiss. He would buy her flowers, write her love letters, and he was always caring, but more than anything, he helped her build a life. He sacrificed to take care of us. Dinners and candlelight are great, but he was the man who stepped up and bought diapers, he was the man who picked me up from day care and made sure I had braces and a bicycle to ride. He was there to help me become a man. Those things, in the grand scheme of things, are way more important than the romance that we find so important when we're young.

Men learn from their mothers—and their fathers—how to act around women. And when I started dating, my mother told me, "You've got to treat a woman the way you would want your father to treat me." From the very beginning of my life, I had two examples of manhood in front of me: my biological father, who didn't treat my mother well; and my father Jaime, who did. I knew right off the bat who I would model myself after.

Women are a driving force in a man's life. Starting as young men, we are motivated by girls. We wake up early on a Saturday, get our hair cut, buy fancy sneakers, and play sports in order to get girls. I may not have the same drive as I did as a teenager when it comes to finding a girlfriend, but I still use my future wife as a motivator. That's one reason I work so hard to establish myself as a businessman and put together a nest egg. Someday I hope to be able to reach a level of comfort that will allow me to spend time with that woman. And a bad breakup also fuels my motivation to be a better person. It prompts me to take a look at how I acted in that relationship, get back in the gym, and become even more successful. Women are frequently my inspiration, and I try to treat them accordingly.

Don't get me wrong—I have some ex-girlfriends who will call me an asshole. But I do my best, following Jaime's example.

My mom also made it clear to me that if a woman didn't respect *herself*, she didn't have the time of day for her. I remember when I was just starting to date as a teenager, a girl showed up at my door wearing heavy makeup and tight clothes, and asking for me. My mom told her I wasn't home and politely shut the door right in her face.

In any case, knowing that my parents have been together for twenty-seven years has shown me that true love exists. It is possible. When you're young you want to date people because of how they look, or how cool they are; but what I've learned from observing my parents is that all those things become irrelevant over time. What matters is the friendship, and the bond, and the loyalty. It's about finding a partner with similar goals, and sticking with them through thick and thin to achieve those goals.

And one last, important thing that my mother taught me about love: You need to value the time you have with the people you care about. At one point, when I was thirteen or fourteen, I asked my mom about the father I'd never met. My mom's reply was that people choose to be in your life, and when they make the decision not to be there, you've got to let them go. "But when they *do* decide to be in your life, make sure you cherish the time you have with them," she continued. "If they mean something to you, you should always let them know it. Because you never know what can happen."

Her words really hit home when I was living in New York and working at BET in my early twenties. I was dating an aspiring French model named Jayla, whom I met at the BET Hip-Hop Awards in 2006. I saw her on the escalator going up as I was going down, and she was so beautiful that I followed her back down just to get her number.

We dated long-distance for a year. It was never a serious relationship, partly because we lived in different countries. I never told her that I loved her, but I always looked forward to her visits. She was full of life, really ambitious, and always a joy to be around. I remember a trip she made to New York in September 2007, almost a year after we'd started dating. I'd just bought my first car, a Cadillac Escalade, and we'd ride up and down the West Side Highway, listening to Kanye West's new album. Her favorite track was "I Wonder," a really inspirational song about following your dreams, and we listened to it over and over.

It was a great visit, but for a variety of reasons, when she was back in the States two months later, we never hooked up. I was overwhelmed with work and dating other women, and it was the holidays. It felt like I had a lot going on, so when she called me to try to get together, I brushed her off. And although we spoke a few times over the holidays, we started to lose touch in the new year. "I'll go visit her when I have a break in March," I kept telling myself.

Valentine's Day came and went and I forgot to hit her up, so I sent her a text the following day, apologizing and letting her know that I wanted to visit soon. She didn't reply. I figured she was upset.

Two weeks later, when I was in a meeting with my boss, Stephen Hill, he asked me, "How are you doing with the Jayla thing? Are you okay?" I just looked at him, totally confused. When he saw my expression, his own face dropped. "I can't believe I'm the one to tell you this," he said, "but she died. She was in a car accident." I sat and stared at him, not quite understanding. I didn't believe it. As soon as I got out of the room I texted her: "Hey, call me back, there's a crazy rumor about you." There was no reply.

When I got home, I looked at her MySpace page, and there it was, clear as day. *Rest in Peace.* I quickly called a mutual friend and learned that Jayla had been coming home from a concert with two friends. She pulled over on the side of the highway in order to switch drivers, and a truck hit her. It broke every bone in her body; she died instantly.

I cried when I heard the story. It was the most devastating conversation I'd ever had. But I didn't know how to talk to anyone about it. Instead, I bottled up my emotions and kept my grief to myself. At home, alone, I played that Kanye West album, listening to "I Wonder" again and again. It was an incomprehensible pain.

I couldn't come to grips with the fact that someone so young and full of life could have everything snatched away from her. I'd had time that I could have spent with her, and I didn't. I had taken that time for granted. I wished I could have it back; and I longed for another chance to tell her what she meant to me. My mom's advice about cherishing the people you love came back to haunt me. Why hadn't I told Jayla what I liked about her? I'd always thought it was corny to tell a woman that I cared about her, especially if we weren't in a serious relationship; but now I regretted it deeply. I would go to sleep with tears in my eyes, wishing that I could tell her how much I'd learned from her, how much I loved her laugh, appreciated her conversation. That I missed her. Sometimes we don't truly appreciate a moment until it becomes a memory, and our moment was snatched away.

One of my favorite movies is *The Life of Pi*—particularly the ending monologue, when the main character explains that of all the hardships he experienced on the lifeboat with that Bengal tiger, the one thing that hurt the most was when they arrived on the shore and the tiger walked off into the woods without looking back to say good-bye. The hardest part of losing someone isn't letting go, but failing to articulate your feelings and get that closure. It's not being able to say good-bye.

Seven years later, the loss of Jayla still hits me hard. Since she died, I can't say I've been perfect with love. I haven't always been honest in relationships. I've cheated, and I'm not proud of it. But one of the things I *am* proud of is that now when I'm with a person, I always let them know how much they mean to me. I'm so thankful for the women that God has sent my way. Every woman I've encountered has made an impact on me. The time I've shared with them has made me smarter and wiser, even if it's just a little bit. And when I'm ready to settle down and marry, the women who have dealt with the bullshit version of me will have helped make me into the man that I hope someday to be—a good husband, a positive father. Thanks to Jayla, I will never again take a relationship or a friendship for granted. My mom was right about that. You never know when a person will walk out of your life. It's important to give them their roses while they're still breathing.

In Her Own Words: Lisa on Love

A new friendship or relationship is a lot like hearing a song for the first time. When you first hear a song, sometimes you fall in love immediately, but sometimes it takes two or three listens and then you fall in love. It's the same when you meet friends or find someone you want to be with—either you fall in love directly or it takes a little time.

After that, if you really like a song, you want to listen to it all the time. It becomes part of your life—you listen to that song when you wake up, on your headphones, when you drive, before you go to bed. It has an intimate place in your life and feels special. But at a certain point, your relationship with the song will shift—maybe the song starts to get popular. Now, the whole world knows that song—it's in the clubs, on the radio, everyone loves it. You hear it too much. Something that was once special to you has become overexposed, and you get a little sick of it.

In relationships that happens as well. When you are in a relationship, or dating someone, in the beginning, it's just you and that person. But over time, as you continue, that tight relationship becomes strained because now your mom, your friends, your coworkers are in the relationship with you. She goes to your work parties, your school friends know her. Now there are other people invested in your relationship, maybe even hating on your relationship—they are part of your world, and as a result your relationship gets pulled in many different directions.

There comes a time when it's smothering and you have to take a step back from it, or stop listening to that song. In friendships, this might mean a big fight, or in relationships a breakup—I need to take a day, a week, time away from the person I once couldn't breathe without.

I've been with my husband for twenty-seven years now. We've always been best friends. And it wasn't always easy—in the beginning it was rough and bumpy.

But going back to that song . . . if it's a song that's meant to be a part of your life—a special song to you—then even after you take your break from it—a day, a month, a year—when you come back to the song you'll still love it. And then you know it's a song meant to be in your life. That's the song that becomes a classic that you'll want played at your wedding. Every time you hear that song for the rest of your life it will bring you back to a special place and make you feel good and warm.

And that's what a real relationship is: It survives; it becomes a classic and it stands the test of time.

Jerry Ferrara Talks About His Mom

Jerry Ferrara is an actor who came to fame as Turtle on the HBO series Entourage. *He has appeared in numerous films and television shows, including* Think Like a Man, Think Like a Man Too, *and the upcoming* Last Vegas, *with Robert DeNiro, Morgan Freeman, and Michael Douglas. His mom raised him and his brother on her own in Brooklyn, New York, after Jerry's father passed away. In this story, he shares how his mother's strength helped make him who he is today.*

My mom is the very definition of strength—the mother bear who takes care of her baby cubs.

My father passed away when I was five. My mom was left with an eight-year-old and a five-year-old—me. My grandparents were scared for her, and wanted her to move back in with them. But she said, "No, I'm gonna do it myself," and went out and got a school crossing-guard job at our grammar school so that she could be near us. She worked her whole life. She didn't date or do anything but raise us kids.

She did everything for us. I still send my mom a Father's Day card, because she was also my father. I remember that when we'd hear a scary noise in the middle of the night, where most kids would go, "Where's Dad to go stop the scary noise!" we'd go wake up our mom instead. She'd go get the bat and creep into the yard to check it out. She always had to be the brave one, to be our first line of defense.

My first love was baseball. When I was seven, I didn't have a father to teach me. My mom, to her credit, did the best she could. She went out and bought a ball and two mitts and watched an instructional video. And then—to my embarrassment—she took me out into the street to play catch with me. She taught me to throw—which is why I throw like a girl!

She instilled in me the knowledge that you can do anything you want in this life. You want to be an actor or an athlete? Well, you breathe the same air as these people. You've just got to want it bad enough. She was a big believer in follow your dreams. So I moved to L.A. when I was nineteen, to pursue acting. She had to put on a tough face, because deep down she was terrified that her son was moving away from everything he knew, but she never let me know how she felt. She later told me that she would cry, she was so worried about me, but she never let me see it, so I was never afraid.

I don't think I would ever have followed my dreams and stuck with them if it wasn't for how she raised me. She gets full, full credit.

3

My Mother's Words of Wisdom About Vision & Fearlessness

When I met up with Tiffany at the center last night, she told me she was starving, so we went down the road to a twenty-four-hour diner for a bite to eat. I watched as she put away a giant strawberry sundae and a cheeseburger with fries, and then eyed the apple pie behind the counter. "I'm already fat anyway, so I might as well enjoy it," she told me. She's exaggerating—at seven months pregnant, she was taking up a whole lot more space in the diner booth, but she wasn't exactly enormous.

She was doing much better than the last time we met; she has that optimistic shine back to her. After a rough winter, Sean shaped up and went and got himself a job—even though it's only part-time, working at a corner deli. But at least he's showing his commitment to the situation and finally has some money coming in. He's even talking about getting them a place together after the baby comes.

But the really good news is that Tiffany has started hearing back from colleges. Unfortunately, she didn't get into her local first choice—Fashion Institute of Technology, in New York City. But she did get accepted by Howard University, an HBCU (historically black college and university) in Washington, D.C., and was even offered a scholarship.

She was incredibly excited—it's a really prestigious college. "I'm just gonna have to get Sean to agree to move down to D.C. with me and the baby. Not that I'd mind getting out of New York City, honestly."

We talked for a while about the expense of life in New York City, and her unhappiness living in a one-bedroom apartment in a not-great housing development with her grandmother. But then she sighed. "Yeah, but D.C. is just so far away. And Sean just finally got a job. How do you uproot three people like that? And then there's the money thing— moving isn't cheap and I still don't know how we're going to cover all the costs of school." She was quiet for a minute, thinking. "I don't know. Maybe it's easier on everyone involved if I just stay here and go to City College or something."

"Is that what you really want?" I asked her.

Her silence was telling. Watching her think it over, I was reminded of my own family's move out of New York City, south to North Carolina.

. . . . .

WHEN I WAS EIGHT years old, a drug dealer named Babyface moved in across the street. Actually, "in" is the wrong word—he wasn't living "in" anything. He had turned a little patch of sidewalk into his office, from which he dealt crack and heroin all day and night long. From the vantage point of our apartment, directly across the street and four stories up, we could watch everything he did. His main office hours were between the hours of midnight and five A.M.—at least, that's when he was most likely to blast hip-hop from his stereo at window-rattling volumes. He turned it off just about the time my parents got up to go to work.

Babyface was a pudgy, round-faced guy—he looked like he was barely out of his teens, hence the nickname. At first, he was only on the street during the weekends, but after a while, he was there every night, surrounded by a posse of Spanish and black thugs. From my bedroom window I had a bird's-eye view of their activities. I would watch the hand-offs happen, over and over—the client rolling up, the slapping of hands, the furtive glance around (though there were never any cops to bust them), and the wads of cash disappearing into Babyface's pocket. I was old enough, by then, to know exactly what was going down.

When we first moved to that block in Woodside, Queens, in

1986, it was a nice, quiet, family-oriented neighborhood. We rented an apartment on the fourth floor of a building owned by a sweet older couple named Harry and Mary. It was a neighborly kind of place—our landlords often babysat me. But by 1990, everything had changed. The drug epidemic in Queens was at its peak, and the whole city was plagued by crime. Nineteen ninety was the most dangerous year in New York history: 2,600 murders—seven a day—and more than 92,000 assaults. The violence was no longer confined to the worst neighborhoods. Even "good" neighborhoods, like ours, had been taken over.

When we'd first moved into our apartment, there were two beat cops that worked our neighborhood, walking the streets every day, deterring crime. By 1990, those two beat cops had retired, and the only police presence was the cruisers that drove through our streets every once in a while. Cop cars were useless when it came to preventing the day-to-day crime that takes place on the sidewalks and in the local housing projects.

Even kids were being targeted by the local criminal elements. I wasn't allowed to ride my bike without an adult alongside me. Junkies would take your sneakers, your backpack, anything of potential value. And then there was the used drug paraphernalia that was dumped all over the streets. It was dangerous to play ball, because you might trip over the syringes and crack vials on the ground.

My mom did her best to shield me from the bad-news characters down on the streets. I remember she kept me really occupied that year, filling every spare moment of my day with productive activities. I was in school, then the after-school program, the school play, swim lessons, summer camp. There wasn't ever any idle time: My parents had me signed up for so many activities that I was too exhausted to go hang out with my friends down in the street. And when I finally got home, there was always an adult around, even though my parents both worked full-time jobs—my grandfather, or Harry and Mary, would always be waiting to keep an eye on me.

Tiffany gave me a funny look. "So, like, they were afraid that you were going to get sucked into the gangster life or something? You were going to, what, go work for Babyface?" She laughed at the improbability of this image.

Hardly. I'd watched Babyface long enough to realize that the life of a low-level drug dealer wasn't much fun. I never saw him pulling up in a nice car, or hanging out with a bunch of girls, and he wasn't covered in chains and jewelry. He was just some dude standing out in the cold in a T-shirt and jeans, pretending that he was doing nothing. His life was not a bit glamorous. Maybe he felt like he was doing what he had to do to take care of his family. But watching him let me know that his path was not the path for me to take.

My mom knew me well enough to know that she didn't have to

worry about me being seduced by the life of crime. What she was really worried about was my physical safety. People were gunned down in Queens all the time, the victims of accidental shootings. Kids were no exception.

One day, my mom took me to a local park to visit the playground. It was one of the few places the kids could safely play—or, at least, it had been until that point. That day, as I was playing on the jungle gym, a vicious pit bull began running loose around the playground. Some drug dealer had decided that our local park, filled with kids, was a good place to let his trained attack dog run around off-leash. A classmate of mine, a sweet little girl, had already been bitten by this dog, and people in the neighborhood were terrified. My mom grabbed me and ran, and we never went back.

That was the final straw. Mom and Jaime decided it was time to get me out of New York. We were living like hostages, afraid to leave our apartment, unable to sleep at night, unable to go to the parks, unable to play normal kid games, unable to even walk across the street safely.

"I kept thinking, 'We have to get him out of this environment,'" my mom tells me. "Kids should be able to run and play and ride their bikes without fear of getting attacked or mugged. They should feel safe playing sports with their friends. We have to get him somewhere he can breathe. Otherwise, he's going to become a statistic; he'll be shot, or worse."

Not long after, my parents packed all of our belongings in a U-Haul, settled me in the backseat of our red Dodge Shadow with our cocker spaniel, Spanky (my mom had already achieved one of her three goals), and set off for a destination five hundred miles south of New York City. We were headed toward a whole new life in North Carolina.

North Carolina wasn't a total shot in the dark: My mother's distant family is originally from there. Specifically, it's the home state of my great-grandma, Mattie Harrison, a strong woman with an entrepreneurial spirit who, I was told, was a bootlegger.

Rocky Mount, North Carolina, where mom's family originally comes from, is a town of roughly 57,000 people on the coastal plains of North Carolina, in Nash County. It also happens to be situated right off Highway 95, at right around the middle point of the East Coast. If you're driving between Miami and New York City, Rocky Mount is your halfway point—just about where you need to stop to spend the night.

This made Rocky Mount the perfect place to be a bootlegger back in the 1930s, and Great-grandma Mattie took full advantage of her situation. She was a grand personality who cooked up moonshine and bootlegged whiskey and sold it to travelers, in between taking care of her eight kids and toiling on her farm and taking in orphans, too. She did pretty well with her endeavors. Her family owned a fair amount of land in rural Nash County, and although my grandmother Helen—Mattie's only daughter, my mom's mom—had eventually moved to New York City, many of my relatives were still there, including my mom's favorite great-uncle Nate. Many of them lived just down the road from each other. It was the kind of place where no one locked the front door.

Not long after the pit bull incident, my parents put me in the car and drove me down to Disney World in Orlando. On the way back, we stopped to visit Great-grandma Mattie. It was my first time out of New York, *and* my first time in the country, and I was totally floored. Great-grandma Mattie had a huge garden, full of trees and flowers and plants I'd never seen before—I knew absolutely nothing about nature, having grown up surrounded by concrete. It was a kind of paradise. I spent three days just playing outside in the garden, riding bikes without concern, making up games with sticks you could just pick up off the ground. That was totally amazing to me.

See, growing up in the city I didn't get to really use my imagination. I was kept busy by the people around me, by toys and books, by scheduled activities, by neighborhood and school friends. But when I stayed at my grandma's house I had nothing to do. I didn't have a brother or sister to play with, and there weren't other kids around, so I had to really come up with my own games. I would play with boxes, or go out to the cotton field behind her house to look at bugs, or do Teenage Mutant Ninja Turtle "kung fu" with sticks. My mom saw me playing outside, having a ball with only my own creativity for company, and decided, right there, that this was the type of environment she wanted me growing up in.

When we got back to the city, she and Jaime took their life savings—a whopping $5,500—and bought an acre of wild land in Rocky Mount. They couldn't afford a house yet, but they decided to move down to the area anyway, in order to start a new life. They believed that the sooner they could get me into a healthier environment, the better.

I am still floored by the amount of vision this took on my mom's part. Think of it: You're just twenty-six, with a little kid, and you decide to buy a piece of grass halfway across the country in a place you've never lived. You don't have a job lined up, no local friends, few family members. Still, my mom was able to look at a plot of empty land and say, "I can see putting a house on this land, putting my family in it, and letting my kid grow up here." That takes an incredible imagination, a whole lot of willpower, and a tremendous amount of guts.

So they packed up that twenty-foot U-Haul truck and caravanned down to Raleigh, using walkie-talkies to keep in touch. Raleigh was an hour east of the property my parents had purchased in Rocky Mount, but it made more sense to live in the city, where there were a lot of job opportunities, than in Rocky Mount, which was fairly economically depressed at the time. They could get established in Raleigh, and when things were more stable, build the house they had always dreamed of. It was a huge risk. Fortunately, my dad found work pretty quickly doing electrical and construction work, and my mom lined up a temp job at the pharmaceutical company Glaxo. The plan was to save every penny they possibly could in order to build that house on our property, and eventually move us to Rocky Mount.

It took almost five years, a time in which we lived very hand to mouth, but Mom and Jaime ultimately did it. Which meant that my mom had achieved her second goal: owning a home.

Tiffany had finished her meal and was eyeing the pies behind the counter. She sat back and looked at me. "Wow, that's crazy," she said. "What if they couldn't find work? You could have ended up homeless."

As my mom told me, "We had the land, so we knew if anything went really wrong we could always pitch a tent. And we made an agreement with each other that if it didn't work, we weren't going to blame each other. We were going to go for it and not look back and let the chips falls where they may. We figured, if you can make it in New York you can make it anywhere, so why not go for it?"

This has always been so inspiring to me. My mom was a rebel; she had a vision and just went for it. She didn't let having a kid stop her from having dreams—in fact, it just made her more focused on achieving the things she had dreamed of. She let my needs motivate her to take the biggest leap you can take. For her, being responsible for me meant her having the vision to try to make a better life—for both of us. After all, it was no better for her living in that environment than it was for me. It was still hard to leave the only city she had ever known, and the life she had built in New York, but New York had changed, and Mom and Jaime knew that North Carolina offered a quality of life that would far outshine the strength of homesickness.

I watched my mom do this crazy, seemingly impractical thing—because she believed she could make it work. And that let me know that anything is possible. If she could take that leap, take those risks, and pursue her dreams—for herself, and for me—then so could I. If she could be that fearless, then so could I. It meant that anything was achievable, as long as I was willing to try.

Mom has said to me, more that once, "What we fear in our minds bears no resemblance to what's really there." She taught me that being afraid of what *could be* is a waste of time. Think big, and don't be afraid to take a leap to make your vision happen.

The point I'm making is that you need to figure out your ideal scenario—and then fight to bring it to reality. What *do* you want? What's your goal for yourself? Your family? To paraphrase the words of Paulo Coelho, "Come up with your personal legend, and even if it seems scary, take the steps that you need to achieve it."

The check had arrived. I paid for Tiffany's meal and then—over her objections—asked the waitress to get her a piece of apple pie to go. "It's for the baby," I said.

She asked for two pieces.

In Her Own Words: Lisa on Vision & Fearlessness

I like to say that fear is *False Evidence Appearing Real*. (I like acronyms!) A lot of times what we invent in our minds has nothing to do with what's really there. We scare ourselves before we've even given ourselves the opportunity to find out what life's about. The monsters in our heads are really just the self-doubt that we bring upon ourselves.

It's really important not to let the fear—fear of what you think might happen—stop you from trying things. Women in particular are intimidated a lot.

My mom held herself back from opportunities because of her fear of the unknown. She'd drive herself crazy with questions like "What if I can't do this? What are people going to think? What are they going to say?"

I have to remind myself, whenever I get scared of trying something new, that it's just the false evidence frightening me. If I remember that, I calm down and I know I can get through whatever I'm facing.

You have to lose the fear if you want to dream big. When Jaime and I decided to move to North Carolina, it was really scary. Here we were with a trailer containing all our belongings in it, moving to another state with nothing but a deed for property in my hand. We had never lived anywhere but New York City.

But we made a pact with each other, before we left, that we would always look forward. Driving our car to North Carolina, the front window view was large, so we kept looking ahead; and the rearview mirror was small, so we only glanced back. We kept our eyes forward, on our vision, and didn't let the fear of what could happen stop us. We just ignored the fear—that False Evidence Appearing Real.

Laz Alonso Talks About His Mom

Laz Alonso has played a wide variety of roles in his celebrated acting career, including stints on Deception, CSI: Miami, *and* Breakout Kings. *His film career includes leads in* Jarhead, Fast & Furious, Stomp the Yard, *and of course* Avatar. *Laz left a career as an investment banker to take a chance on Hollywood, and the risk paid off. Also a fellow BET alum, Laz told me how tough his mom was in this story.*

Growing up, my mother had to be my mother and my father, because my father died at a very early age. He was in and out of rehab because of alcoholism. He would go away, get cleaned up, come home, and be out again that weekend. That was our reality from early on. So my mother did the heavy lifting, and she busted her butt to get me through school.

I remember one story from when I was young. I had a Green Machine—this kid's bike that was kind of like a hybrid Big Wheel. I was the only kid on the block who had one. But there was a kid who was the neighborhood bully, and he wanted one. He was named Fred. One day he came up and snatched my Green Machine away from me.

Most other kids would have run home to get their older brother or sister to come help them out, do their dirty work for them. But I was an only child, so I always went to my mom. My mom was no joke. She feared no one.

That day, I ran home to her and said, "Yo, Mom! Fred took my Green Machine! Let's go beat him up!"

But my mom didn't even let me in the house. She just stood there in the doorway and slapped me across the face. I couldn't believe it. And then she asked, "Did Fred hit you as hard as I just did?"

I started crying, but she just repeated the question: "Who hit you harder? Me or Fred?"

And I went, "You did!"

"Well, if you don't want me to hit you again then you got to go out there and get that Green Machine back, because I worked too hard to buy it for you." She meant it, too. So I turned around and went back to Fred. I didn't say a word. I just started whaling on him. I was taking karate at the time, and I went at him so fast that you couldn't tell if it was my hands or feet flying. He didn't know what was coming.

"I want my Green Machine back," I yelled. And he gave it back to me.

When I went back to my mom, with the Green Machine, she said, "Don't ever let anyone take anything away from you again. What's yours is yours, what's theirs is theirs." It taught me a valuable lesson— that I was the man of the house, I had to protect not just what was mine, but what was *ours*. She'd worked too hard for our life. It was when I knew, as the saying goes, *that shit is real*. That this was real life.

Fred and I ended up becoming best friends after the Green Machine. Twenty years later I ran into Fred at an IHOP, and we had a great laugh about it.

This experience with my mom and Fred didn't make me violent. It didn't turn me into a bully or make me fight more, but it *did* teach me to respect what you have, stand up for yourself, and how to earn respect from others. And after that I became very intolerant of bullies. It made me have empathy for people who *were* bullied—I would befriend them, help them not get bullied. The bullies usually gave them a pass when I was around, because I tried to get along with everyone.

These days, I never take anyone for granted. It doesn't matter their color, creed, religion, sexual preference, handicap: It's *who* they are, not *what* they are, that's important. If you are the only person who *isn't* judging someone when everyone else is, someday that's the person who will be by your side when you need it the most.

That's the theme of my life. Judge me for who I am, not what I am.

4

My Mother's Words of Wisdom About Hustle & Ambition

I hadn't heard from Tiffany in several months, but I'd been thinking about her a lot. Word on the street was that she'd given birth to a healthy baby boy named Tyler, just three days after finishing her high school finals. I'd sent over a card and a gift for the baby, and she'd texted me a snapshot of Tyler in return. But I hadn't seen her around the Boys & Girls Club—it wasn't too surprising, since she had a baby to take care of—but I worried about how she was handling life with a newborn.

So I was thrilled to hear her voice on the other end of the line one afternoon in early summer. In the background, I could hear the faint cooing of a baby.

Tiffany told me all about the birth—more, frankly, than a single guy in his twenties really wants to hear. It sounded kind of like hell. But she was proud of herself for having done it.

"I didn't know I was that strong," she said. "And Tyler—wow, he's just incredible. Seriously, my heart explodes every time I look at him."

As for Sean—well, he showed up for the birth. And it sounded like he was coming around to visit them every evening, bringing groceries and things for the baby. But the idea of moving in together has been dropped—too expensive—and his contributions to the cost of the baby have been negligible, at best. A few bucks here or there, not nearly enough to cover the expenses of baby gear and formula and diapers. And more diapers. And more diapers.

"So many diapers," she groaned. "I love this little guy, but sometimes it's like all he does is poop and eat and cry. It's just me and him and the diapers, all day long. Honestly, as much as I love him, I'm kind of looking forward to starting college in the fall and being around adults again."

"So you're going to do it? You're moving to D.C. to go to Howard?"

"I think so. Maybe. I hope so." She stopped and made a funny sound.

"What's that?"

"The baby. I think he's smiling." Her voice got soft, and I could hear her cooing to the baby. "Are you smiling at your momma, little man?"

Aww. Even I felt a little choked up. "Are you happy?"

"Yeah," she said. "Definitely. I mean—maybe I'm a little bored sometimes, being here all by myself. Mostly I'm just worried about money. I'm down to the last five bucks in my bank account.

"Sean says his friend might be giving him a job at his club. And I've *got some ideas. I mean, it's not like I can go back to waitressing at the diner. But I thought—maybe I can set up an Etsy store or something? I can do some sewing while Tyler sleeps, and try to sell my stuff online. I can do it anywhere—here or at college. Plus, it's a good way to get my design ideas out there. What do you think?"*

"I think that's pretty resourceful," I said. "That's exactly the kind of hustle my mom would approve of."

"You think so?"

I knew so. Be creative, try new things, and explore your passions—but most important, don't be afraid to think big. That's what my mom always taught me.

WHEN I WAS FOURTEEN, in 1996, I was convinced that my life's calling was to be a rapper, an actor, or a Supreme Court justice (don't laugh). I would watch Will Smith on *The Fresh Prince of Bel Air* and think "I want to be like him," even though I had no idea what that actually meant. It was the era of Tupac and Biggie. For the teenage boys of Raleigh, where I was now a freshman at Sanderson High School, it was all about the bling and the baggy jeans, about being "hardcore" despite the fact that you had only recently stopped wearing superhero underwear.

I was no exception to the rule. My freshman year of high school marked the beginning of my—mercifully brief—rebellious phase.

We had only recently moved to the area, so I still didn't have many friends. I wanted to look cool, to fit in, but when I hit high school I couldn't figure out the best way to do that. I wore the fake gold chains and the baggy clothes, and tried my best to be cool. I spent hours coming up with rhymes; I drank and I smoked; I tried marijuana. I pretended I was tougher than I was in order to hang out with the wrong crowd. I thought I was a real cool kid.

My mother, not surprisingly, was not amused. She wasn't amused when I broke my curfew; she wasn't amused when I wore my jeans hanging halfway to my knees, and she certainly wasn't amused when I told her my new ambition in life. "I'm going to be a rapper," I announced to her.

For the first time in her life, my mother wasn't particularly encouraging. She hated the profanity of rapping. Worse, I rapped about the things that I'd witnessed growing up in New York City. That was not the life she wanted for me (the life she'd moved to North Carolina in order to escape), and she didn't like hearing me glorify it. "This isn't the move for you," was her reply. "You really want to do this? We'll support you. But this isn't it for you."

I was still convinced that it was. And I just *knew* that my big break was going to be at the Sanderson High talent show. Apparently, there was a "talent scout" coming down from New York for the event in order to look for the next great rap star, or at least that's what the flyers said. I spent weeks working on my rhymes and getting ready for the show. I thought I had nailed it: I had visions of being whisked off to a recording studio straight from the high school auditorium.

But when I actually stepped onto the stage that day, I was completely unprepared for how hard it would be to perform. The music was louder than I expected. The lights and the crowd and the sound of my tape blaring over the speakers disoriented me. You can probably guess what happened: I bombed. I was so bad that my classmates actually booed me off the stage.

Despite her quiet objections to my hip-hop aspirations, my mom was in the audience that day, along with Jaime. And even as everyone else around her was jeering, she was applauding as loudly as she could. It was one thing I could always count on: No matter what I chose to pursue, she was guaranteed to be cheering me on, always my number one fan, even if it was embarrassing for both of us.

After all, this wasn't the first time she'd sat in an audience and watched me perform. From the moment that I was capable of expressing my own interests, my mom was encouraging me to pursue them. She gave me the space and time to explore whatever caught my attention, always urging me to be creative. She was constantly telling me that I was special, gifted, chosen, that I could do anything I wanted to do. She'd always simply say, "Go get 'em."

And so, with her encouragement ringing in my ears, I *would* go for it, whatever struck my interest at the time. When I was six years old, it was acting. I played P. T. Barnum in a stage rendition of *The Greatest Show on Earth* in a school production. My mother's first words when she came backstage? "You're a star."

At seven years old, it was singing. I somehow found myself belting out the national anthem when David Dinkins became the mayor of New York City. (The fact that I knew all the words to the national anthem by heart? That was also my mom's doing.) "You're amazing," she told me.

After we moved to North Carolina, it was sports. The whole family would get up at the break of dawn so that I could go play Mighty Mite football with the Green Road Eagles. I was skinny and small, and would get hit so hard that I'd almost black out. But still, my mom would be applauding from the sidelines.

And then it was basketball.

And then it was rapping.

Along the way, my parents always supported my ambitions, no matter how often they changed or how unlikely they were. They never missed a performance, a game, a tournament. They were completely behind me—even if they didn't particularly care for what I was doing.

The Sanderson High Talent Show was the first and last time I would ever publicly perform as a rapper. Not long afterward, my mother sat me down to have a heart-to-heart about my ambitions. Her advice was circumspect, but cut straight to the point: "Whatever you want to do when you grow up, just make sure you're the best at it," she told me.

In the years since, I've thought a lot about those words. The truth is, you'll probably have a lot of different ambitions over the course of your life. It's up to you to take an honest look in the mirror and assess your strengths and weaknesses. If you're not really outstanding at basketball, at some point you've got to say to yourself, "It might be time to give up my dream of being in the NBA." But just because you haven't been given the ability to play basketball doesn't mean you can't be a coach, be an assistant, or get a team ring. There are so many people, beyond just players, involved in any championship. As I'd later learn working at NASCAR, only one person can drive the race car, but the people on the pit crew, the marketing director, the medical assistant—everyone on that team—gets to hold the trophy. Just because you may not have the talent to be the artist to pay the bills doesn't mean you can't live in the world of what you love. So you love basketball? Maybe it's time to shift your goals to being a sports announcer or the person who designs the jerseys, even a team owner. Use your passion within the skill set that you actually possess.

Not long after that disastrous talent show, I gave myself a good hard look in the mirror and admitted that I wasn't very good at rapping. I wasn't ever going to be the guy making the music. But I also realized that I still loved music, and wanted to be part of that world. How could I be involved in the industry without being an actual artist? Where did my talents truly lie?

Fourteen may be an early age to be thinking about your career trajectory, but my parents had set the bar high. From the time I was little, my mother had instilled in me the importance of a strong work ethic, and the importance of ambition.

Just because my mom only finished two years of Hunter College didn't mean she didn't have drive and professional aspirations. When we arrived in North Carolina, despite a lack of job prospects, my mom immediately found temp work at the pharmaceutical company Glaxo, and within three months she'd talked them into hiring her full time. For the next twelve years, she worked there as an administrator.

Soon after they arrived in North Carolina, my parents also identified an opportunity in the local contracting industry: There was only one concrete-cutting company in the region, and it would only take big jobs. So Jaime started up a company that he called Coremaster, specializing in concrete cutting, hole drilling, and controlled demolition, and began methodically pursuing the smaller jobs that were still available. He worked days at Coremaster, building up his fledgling business, and then did temp work at night to help pay the bills.

I watched my parents hustle all throughout my junior and high school years. They often worked two or three jobs at a time— besides her job at Glaxo, my mother also did invoicing work for

Coremaster on the weekends. My mother traveled an hour and a half each way to her day job, and never complained. They were driven: to build their own business, to make enough money to provide me with everything I needed, to find the money to build that house my mom had always dreamed off.

By 2003, my mom felt that she'd hit a plateau at Glaxo—she wasn't learning anything new, and nothing frustrates my mom more than feeling like she isn't growing. So when the company went through a corporate merger and offered buyout packages to long-time employees, she saw an opportunity. She would go work alongside my dad, to help grow Coremaster. She accepted a package and began a new career as one of the few female minority contractors in North Carolina, and the *only* one doing concrete cutting.

Going to work for yourself is incredibly risky. It's one of the most challenging things you can do. When you work for yourself there's no set paycheck. In thirty days if you don't have a job lined up and money coming in, the lights go out, the phone gets shut off, the bills go unpaid. It's a lot of pressure, and certainly one of the scariest things you can do in life. But you already know how my mom feels about fear: She was absolutely fearless. As she puts it, "Self-employment shows you what you're made of."

Her drive has always inspired me. "I am very ambitious," she has told me. "You give me an opportunity and I'm going to take it and run with it." No matter where she was working, she was always seeking to grow her career. At Glaxo, she was constantly taking every class that the company regularly offered; sitting in on skill-learning seminars even when there was no room left in the class. And once she made the move to Coremaster, she decided to go back to school to learn more about contracting. She attended a six-month contractor's construction course—a kind of mini-degree offered by the University of North Carolina. It was a grueling course and a long drive from home, but she stuck to it. My mom learned how to read blueprints, write contracts, and bid projects. She was never afraid to roll up her sleeves and get dirty; she even went out to construction sites to get experience in the field. In the middle of a burning-hot summer, my tiny mother was mounting these giant machines to walls and cutting bricks, hauling concrete to Dumpsters—all in addition to hitting the books. When it was done she got a certificate, and we couldn't have been more proud.

My mom also knew how to be responsible and conservative with her money. "Invest in yourself, and invest in land," she would tell me. "You can trust yourself more with money than in a company you know nothing about; and invest in land because it's the only thing they aren't making more of." And sure enough, by the time I was a sophomore in high school, they had saved enough money to build the house in Rocky Mount, and we finally moved there from Raleigh.

As I grew older, my mom's drive became my drive. Her hustle

became my hustle. If she was going to work multiple jobs in order to get ahead in life, so was I. To this day, I still can't sleep—I have a real fear that if I'm sleeping, my competition is working. I know Diddy is somewhere in the world putting together a business deal, and I don't want to get caught kicking my feet up. I work multiple jobs simultaneously: In an average day I'll do a TV show, a voice track for a radio show, memorize lines for an upcoming film, and piece together a marketing plan for a Crown Royal event. I do all this while trying to balance a social life, hit the gym, and find time to watch an episode of *Homeland* before getting in a few hours of sleep and doing it all over again. And I've been doing this since I turned fifteen. This type of hectic schedule keeps me sane. It's the only thing I know.

"I'm not sleeping, either, but that's not because I'm working three jobs," Tiffany said.

"Having a newborn baby is kind of like having three jobs," I replied.

That summer, the summer I was fifteen, we had finally landed in Rocky Mount. By that point my family had moved twice in Raleigh, following the growth of my parents' business, going wherever their work took us. But now we were finally in the home they had hustled so hard to build. It took almost my whole life for them to build it, and now I had only three years left to live there. It was a one-level ranch-style home with four bedrooms and two bathrooms. The house wasn't huge, but it had an enormous backyard. My mom painted the facade a soft yellow called "Casablanca" and I helped my dad lay the stone path that led to the front door.

By the time we moved to Rocky Mount, I was already in tenth grade. When I arrived at Northern Nash High School, most of the kids already had their crews. I was never good in large groups anyway, and now I found it nearly impossible to make friends. I'd played basketball in middle school, and still held out hopes of being a basketball star, but the fact that I was skinny and short was finally catching up with me. When I tried out for the high school basketball team, I didn't make the cut. Rejected and lonely, I felt like an outcast.

When I first arrived in Rocky Mount, I hadn't learned to appreciate it yet. My goal was to leave. How was I going to get out?

The answer: work. By the summer of my sophomore year, I had three jobs lined up.

I'd be lying if I said that my early ambition was at the scale of what it is today. I was fifteen. Mostly I wanted money to put in the old red 1989 Dodge Shadow that my mom let me drive with my new learner's permit. I wanted to be cool with girls. I wanted to be able to visit my old friends and family in New York City, and buy hip-hop mix tapes at swap meets. And I wanted to fill the hours that other people filled with friends and sports, because I didn't have much of either in my life.

The first job I got was at Foot Locker. By that point, I already had a thing for sneakers—and, well, we all know how pricey sneakers can be. An employee discount seemed like an opportunity I shouldn't pass up. So I headed down to the local mall, walked into Foot Locker, and talked the manager into giving me a job.

Next, I walked down the mall to another store, called Kaemin's, which carried all the cool clothes in town. Soon, I was working there, too. That summer, I often worked a double shift: I'd punch in at the clothing store at eight A.M., and then start my shift at Foot Locker at five P.M.

My goal at the time may have just been to make money and get girls, but I was starting a habit that I still have to this day: balancing multiple jobs. Growing up, I'd heard my mom talk about why she worked multiple jobs: It wasn't just about the money and her drive to get ahead, but about job security. "Always make sure you have more than one revenue stream," she'd tell me. "Don't put yourself in a position where one person's attitude can dictate your career, success, and financial stability." That summer I started following her example. And it worked in my favor: If one job cut my hours because they had a slow week, I had another job to fall back on.

I didn't always handle my new responsibilities well. That summer was the first—and last—time that I stole something. I nicked a pair of white Air Jordans that I thought were really fresh. It was a bad call: I couldn't even wear them. I spent most of my day at the mall, and was paranoid that people there would know that I couldn't afford Air Jordans. Instead, I hid those shoes under the bed. When I finally pulled them out, to wear to a school dance, I had a date with good ol' karma. A fight took place at the dance that night; the police arrived and sprayed mace. We all ran out of the gym, and my first step was into a big pile of mud that was waiting outside for me. My shoes that started out white and fresh were soiled and muddy by the end of the night. I learned a valuable lesson: Nothing in life is free. Even if you don't get caught, it will come back to haunt you. As my mom likes to put it, "Things always find a way to come full circle," and this episode really brought that lesson home.

In any case, the third job I got that summer—the job that would shape my career—was the most important job of all.

Soul 92 Jams—WRSV at 92.1 on the dial—is Rocky Mount's top R&B, hip-hop, and soul station. It was the sound track to my life back then. So when station owner Chuck Johnson and afternoon DJ Derrick "D-Train" Alston walked into Foot Locker one afternoon, I knew exactly who they were. They'd come to the mall to do a radio remote, and when they came into the store where I was working, one of the other salespeople gave me a nudge.

"Rap for them and maybe they'll put you on the radio," he whispered.

Yes, my coworkers had heard about my rap dreams, and at that point, I still harbored delusions about a hip-hop career. So I started rapping for Chuck and D-Train, right in the middle of Foot Locker.

Chuck laughed. "Honestly? You're not the best rapper," he said. "But you got a great voice. Why don't you come down to the radio station some time?"

So I did. By the end of that month, I was spending my weekends interning for D-Train and Chuck, learning everything that happens behind the scenes at a radio station. D-Train had a gig I really admired. Working only four hours a day and DJ-ing the afternoon show, he made good money, had a nice car, and tons of respect. I thought it was the coolest thing in the world that people asked him to host parties. You could get *paid* to drink free drinks and hang out with girls? Suddenly, I had a new goal: *I have to work on the radio and be the afternoon drive-time DJ.*

Within three months I had wiggled my way into hosting my own show on Sunday afternoons.

Radio was different back then: I had a lot of creative freedom, and I took full advantage of my love of music. For six hours every Sunday afternoon, I hosted a show called Sizzling Sundays, playing Aaliyah, Jah Rule, LL Cool J, and anything else that was hot at the time. For those six hours, I wasn't high school junior Terrence Jenkins; I was Youngest in Charge, Terrence J—first name and initial only, just like all the other DJs.

My mom's words—"Whatever you want to do when you grow up, just make sure you're the best at it"—finally hit home. Not long after I sat in the DJ booth for the first time, any desire to be a rapper disappeared. I had a real knack for being on the radio, just being an announcer and talking, and it was clear that I was a mediocre musician at best. My passions simply shifted; I wanted to focus all my energy on becoming an on-air personality now.

My mom was supportive. She began filling her personal Terrence J museum with tape recordings of every on-air show I hosted. To her credit, she gave me an enormous amount of leeway and flexibility to pursue my new interest. Suddenly, at age seventeen, I was out late doing radio remotes at nightclubs. Not every mom would give that the okay. But my mom offered me the freedom that I needed to grow in my ambitions—while at the same time giving me boundaries within which I needed to operate. She always made sure I got home on time.

At Christmas and Thanksgiving, when—as the youngest, newest talent at the station—I had to come in and cover everyone else's shifts, she and Jaime would come down to the station with me. They'd sit there in the DJ booth, wearing headphones so they could listen to the show. And we'd celebrate the holidays right in the middle of the radio station: string bean casserole, candied yams with marshmallow topping, mac and cheese.

Their support and encouragement helped me grow for three years at Soul 92 Jams, and the opportunities I had there ultimately led to the career that I have now. I'd found the thing I was best at, and I never looked back.

"I can't believe that you were fifteen and you had your own radio show." Tiffany sounded shocked. *"That would never happen in New York."*

When I was fifteen, I may have desperately wanted to leave Rocky Mount, but in retrospect, I'm really happy my mom moved us there. It's true—the decision to raise me in a small town ultimately gave me far more career opportunities than I would have had if I'd stayed in New York City, or even Raleigh. In a big city, there's big competition early on: The application line for the Foot Locker in Times Square goes down the block. I may never have gotten a job there. And DJ-ing an afternoon shift at the local commercial radio station? In a big city? Crickets.

In Rocky Mount, I was an ambitious fish in a small pond, able to get all the work experience I wanted, working with people who were happy to nurture me. In life, things aren't always in the order you want them, but you have to follow God's plan. Sometimes you just have to make the best of your environment. Whether you're in the biggest city or the smallest town in the world, there are opportunities everywhere. It's up to you to find and take advantage of them.

That was the opportunity that my mom unknowingly gave me. But what she also gave me was natural ambition. I inherited that from her; I was *born* with it.

The result of my mom's encouragement was that I was always thinking big. The second I walked into the door of a new job, I would be analyzing who was doing what, and what it meant. And then I would try to figure out how I, too, could get to the top of that food chain. What did it take to be the absolute best at what I was doing? It didn't matter if it was a minimum-wage job: The minute I walked into Foot Locker, my goal was being Employee of the Month by selling the most sneakers, and eventually owning my own Foot Locker. And then, once I got on air at Soul 92 Jams, it was moving from a weekend show to a coveted day shift. I was always looking up. I was always looking for the next opportunity.

In life, you're going to hit stumbling blocks. It happens to everyone. What's important is what you do after you hit that stumbling block. Do you give up and sulk? Or do you find another path? Do you keep looking up, and try to find a new way to get there?

After you get told no, what happens next is really up to you. The person who tells you no doesn't have that power. They may be blocking that opportunity, but your attitude toward that no is what's going to shape your life. If you have a negative attitude about being defeated, not getting a job, getting cut from a team—if you take those life failures and sit in a corner and mope, decide not to put yourself out there anymore—then nothing good will ever happen to you. That energy is very transferable. But if you take that no and use it as an opportunity to figure out what you really want to do with yourself? That's how you make real progress in your life.

In Rocky Mount, I was horribly embarrassed that I didn't make the basketball team. All the cool kids played basketball and football, but I was too short for basketball and too skinny for football. Instead, I found something different. Radio was unique and special; soon, people would look at me and say, "That's the guy from the radio." That was my in.

If I'd been playing basketball I might not have found the radio station; and if I hadn't found the radio station I might not have chosen the path my life has taken. Honestly, even if I'd made the basketball team, I never would have made it to the NBA. But that job at Soul 92 Jams? The hustle that I learned from my mom? The drive that pushed me to find the thing I truly was "best" at? That is what made me the man I am today.

In Her Own Words: Lisa on Hustle & Ambition

Ambition and hustle are the mothers of invention. You have to find your own opportunities. Scholarships that are available to pay for school. Services that no one else is offering. You should never sit back and wait for the phone to ring. You need to be on the grind, as we say; looking for that next opportunity. Constantly trying to move forward.

Hustle is having to chase the things you want. You have to be dedicated to put in the work that it takes to get there and stay there. If given an opportunity, you need to seize it and go for it with full gusto. And when the opportunity is not there you have to go find one. Blaze your own trail.

Right now we have really high unemployment in America. So maybe you'll have to create your own job. Find something people have a need for and create it yourself. Like our company, Coremaster—we were blazing our own trail. When we moved to North Carolina, we found that the only concrete-cutting company here was really big, and wouldn't do small jobs. But we were happy to take those small jobs, give customers an option for small projects. And now we have fifty-eight clients. We blazed a trail that wasn't here, made our own opportunity.

Anyone can have ambition, but if you're going to make things happen, you need to hustle, too. People can move mountains with their mouths. But what is it that you're really doing? We can say "Oh yeah, I'm gonna do this!" but are you really putting in the time and work?

I'm more of an action person than a talking person. Talk is cheap. What's the plan to put things into action? The hardest thing in life is starting something and getting it completed. The best way to get it done is to show it, not talk about it. What you do tells the world who you are and what you're really about.

If I give you my word I'm going to do something, I always follow through.

Ludacris Talks About His Mom

Christopher "Ludacris" Bridges is a Grammy Award–winning rapper, celebrated actor, and entrepreneur. One of the most influential musicians to come out of the South, he has also appeared in numerous films, including *Hustle & Flow, Crash, and the extremely successful* Fast & Furious *franchise. Here he shares how his mom's hustle taught him the value of working hard.*

I get a lot of miles in terms of hustle from my mom. She had me when she was in college, and she was still working two jobs, at a grocery store and as a real estate agent. She led by example: I knew she was hardworking, and anything less was just not accepted around the household. She was a supermom. I couldn't fathom how she was doing all that stuff at once.

I remember her graduating from college. Mothers are always proud of their sons, but it's very rare when you take a moment and say you are proud of your mom. And then she went back, fifteen years later, and got her business graduate degree, and I was even more proud. It motivated me, and let me know that there's no limitations on what you can do. And it's never too late to get something done.

I used to get whupped a lot, for things like pitching pebbles at a neighbor's window to get their attention and accidentally breaking it. My mom would make me go outside and pick a branch or stick out of the tree; if it was too skinny, she'd tell me that it wasn't big enough and make me go back and get another one. That pretty much set me on the path, right there.

I can honestly say that your parents have to put fear in your heart, of doing something you're not supposed to do. It helps you think twice about right and wrong, about your morals.

The most important thing she did, though, was that as I was growing up, once a year she made me write down my goals, what I wanted to accomplish and achieve the next year. It put me in the mind-set of practicing going after what I wanted. I hated doing it at the time; I didn't understand it until years later. But it's a reason that I'm so driven. If I have dreams and goals now, I write them down in my head and I go after them.

I remember what my mom used to say to me: "It can work, if you work it."

5

My Mother's Words of Wisdom
About the Importance of Learning

*T*yler is a cute, chubby baby boy—all cheeks. He is, as Tiffany
*promised, pretty incredible, a happy-go-lucky little guy. She
brought him over to the Boys & Girls Club last night to show*
him off to the staff and mentors. The whole place was buzzing over that
baby, passing him around and around until he finally started crying
for his momma. Tiffany tucked him up against her chest and soothed
him like a pro. Hard to believe she's only been doing this for three
months.

As for Tiffany—well, she'd lost most of the baby weight but she
didn't look like herself. It was the first time I'd seen her in sweat-
pants, and without makeup. She looked exhausted and older than
her age, a tired mom rather than the fashion-forward teen I remembered. Understandable. Still, despite her game smile as she held Tyler,
I couldn't shake the feeling that something important had shifted.

I pulled her aside and asked what was wrong.

"What do you mean? Everything's great. Just look at him."

"He's amazing." And then, I couldn't help myself. "But what about you? You're feeling good? All set to start college next month? Got the move figured out?"

"Oh, yeah. That." She shrugged, pulled out her cell phone and studied a text she'd just received. "Right. I don't think it's going to happen. I mean, I needed to register a few weeks ago and I didn't."

Not what I'd hoped to hear. "Why not?"

"There's just no way," she said. She typed a quick response on her phone and then tucked it back in her pocket. "It's time to get real about it."

"Says who?"

"Well, for one, Sean won't move. Says he's only now getting it going in New York and he doesn't want to have to start over down there. Plus, all his friends are here. I kind of see his point."

"I'm sure there are jobs in D.C., too. And you don't necessarily have to go with him."

She ignored this. "You know, he's actually a great dad? I didn't know what to expect, but he's great. He takes him for walks and down to his basketball games in the park, shows him off to his friends. He loves Tyler. So maybe he's not so good at, you know, punching in a time card. There are other things that are important, right? It just means that

I have to go get a job instead. But maybe that's the sacrifice that I'm supposed to make. You were talking about sacrifices before, remember?"

"Right, right." I winced. I'd been talking about giving up partying, not giving up school. "But having to get a job doesn't mean that you can't still try to go to college."

"Maybe." Tyler let out a sudden wail and she jiggled him a little bit, not meeting my eyes. "Sean says there's really no point in going to college anyway. It's not the real world. It's a waste of time and money to sit in rooms and learn about stuff dead people did."

"That's not all you learn. You know that."

She shrugged. "Maybe I just think I have to go because everyone told me I could. Is college really that important? Maybe it's more important to be here, with my family. If we can't pay the rent who cares how much I know about art history or geology." She brightened her voice. "Honestly, we're all better off here. This is the right way."

My heart sank. I couldn't help thinking that my mom would have hated to hear Tiffany talk like this. Even though she made the difficult decision to drop out of college in order to take care of me, my mother never stopped striving to finish her own education. And from the day I was born, her number one priority for me was helping me get to college.

But I could remember, too, how pointless higher education sometimes seemed to me when I was in high school. It was only because of my mom that I was ultimately convinced of the importance of learning—and it ended up being one of the best decisions of my life. So it seemed like Tiffany could use the same sort of pep talk my mom used to give me.

On the day that I graduated from North Carolina A&T State University, in 2004, I stood onstage in front of the entire college student body and gave my mom my college ring.

On that bright June day, I stood in front of two thousand seniors and their families, and held up my college ring. "My mom sacrificed everything so I could be here. She didn't get to go to prom, because of me. She didn't get to graduate from college, because of me. She dedicated her entire life to making a better life for her son, and to making sure that I would be able to get this college degree. The symbol of that degree is this ring, and so she deserves it more than anyone else." I called her up onstage and, as she cried with happiness, I handed the ring to her. I'd had it engraved with her and Jaime's initials: TO LG, JG.

I've never seen my mom so proud in my life. To this day, she wears that ring alongside her wedding and engagement bands. She tells me that it was one of the best days of her life. She had officially achieved all her goals.

In a lot of ways, her plan to get me to go to college was present in my life long before I even know what college was. For instance, she shared with me her love of reading. Ever since I can remember, my mom has given me books for Christmas. Often, they are inspirational books, taking cues from my ambitions—like *Images of Movie Stars* or *501 Movie Stars*—and sometimes they are educational—like *Porto Rico: The Story of Puerto Rico* when I expressed an interest in learning more about where Jaime's family came from.

In the front flap of the book, my mom always puts a bookplate embossed with our family crest—a picture of a sailing ship—and the words *Ex Libris Terrence H. Jenkins*. Underneath that, my mom will always write a dedication, something like this:

TODAY I THOUGHT ABOUT YOU

AND HOW PROUD I AM

OF YOU FOR BEING SUCH A <u>GOOD</u> PERSON.

I REALIZED THAT MY DREAMS FOR YOU CAME TRUE

AND OTHERS WILL SEE

WHAT I HAVE ALWAYS KNOWN

YOU ARE AN <u>EXTRAORDINARY</u> PERSON.

AND AS YOU CONTINUE TO GROW

PLEASE REMEMBER ALWAYS

HOW VERY MUCH

I LOVE YOU.

. . . LOTS OF LOVE, MOM, 12/2010

Thanks to her, I grew up loving to read, even when I was just memorizing the words of *Goose Goofs Off* as it was read out loud to me. To me, books are windows into a different world. That's how you grow as a person, that's how you absorb more of the world.

I think my mom focused so much on reading because she'd never been able to go back to college to finish her degree. That always bothered her. Despite all the things she'd achieved with her life, she felt like she'd missed out on opportunities because she didn't have a diploma. Even within Glaxo, she wasn't able to apply for open job positions that interested her because the job description required a college degree.

IT'S NO WONDER THAT she focused so much on getting me to go to college. From the time I was old enough to understand what "college" was, I heard that if I wanted to get a good job and keep it, I had to take my education as far as I could. "I don't ever want a door to be closed to you," she would tell me. "Opportunities will come to you once you have a degree."

Because of her, I always knew that school was important: a privilege and a tool, rather than a chore. In elementary school, I never wanted to miss a day. I would hear stories of kids across the world who weren't able to get an education and realized that I was lucky to be able to learn as much as I wanted.

School was also an escape—especially in New York City, where the neighborhood was so tough. As an only child, it was also the only place where I saw people my own age. My friends were there. And girls! I couldn't fathom why the young guys in my neighborhood didn't want to go to school: That's where the smartest, prettiest girls were. It struck me that it took just as much effort to goof off as it did to learn. There were kids who were so creative in coming up with notes and excuses to get out of class; if they'd put half of that focus on their schoolwork, they'd have done a lot better.

That's not to say that I was totally focused on schoolwork. In all honesty, I excelled academically in elementary and middle school, but by the time I hit high school, my grades were average at best. I'd spent so much time focusing on my work at the radio station that, despite my enthusiasm for attending school, I hadn't always been as dedicated to my homework as I should have been. I did well at the things I could talk my way out of—English, Social Studies, Debate, Arts & Crafts, Gym—but I struggled in Math and Science. In those classes, you either know what you're talking about or you don't.

By my senior year, I'd already been working at Soul 92 Jams for three years. With graduation approaching, my plan was to try to work for the radio station full time. All of seventeen years old, this sounded like a dream come true. I remember thinking: *What I want to do for the rest of my life is radio, and I already have that opportunity here—so why do I need to go to college?*

When I told my mom that this was what I was thinking, she was not happy. "Baby, I never got the opportunity to go to college," she said. "I wanted it more than anything in the world. So it would mean the world to me if you went. If you think that the job opportunities that you have now are amazing . . . just imagine how much better they will be after college. Just give me this one thing."

I was finally beginning to grasp how many sacrifices she had made on my behalf. All the opportunities I'd taken for granted— prom, college, first dates, and freedom—she'd missed out on because she was taking care of me. Once I finally understood this, my perspective on college changed a bit. Going to college wasn't just about me; it was also about her. I wanted to make her proud.

I ended up applying to a bunch of colleges—Howard, the University of Carolina at Chapel Hill, a few colleges in New York City—but from the get-go, I knew that where I really wanted to go was North Carolina A&T State University. I'd already visited the campus a few times with my friend Eric, whose sister Michelle went there; I'd even attended an A&T homecoming. It was a beautiful campus, it was affordable due to in-state tuition, and it was close enough to my parents that I could drive home for the weekend and steal food.

Most important, they accepted me.

Not long after I got my acceptance letter, my mom and I drove three hours east, to Greensboro, North Carolina, to visit the campus.

My first stop—before I even met any of the professors—was the radio station. We'd arranged to meet the program director, a woman named Cherié Lofton, and when I walked in I went straight up to her and introduced myself. "Hi, my name is Terrence. I know how to use Cool Edit Pro"—a top software audio program—"and I really want to work here. Are there any opportunities?" Then I handed her my air check—a recording of my best breaks, like an audio résumé.

I was definitely a young lion. Cherié and I can laugh at it now, but I was very confident and sure of myself. I knew exactly what I wanted to do; and sure enough, before I'd even started my freshman year, Cherié had me on the air. In fact, my very first day of college, I hosted the big freshman step show; and for the next four years, I hardly stopped to put down the microphone. Working at Soul 92 Jams would have been great, but I would have missed out on maximizing my full potential and seeing what else the world had to offer. My mom was right—I was getting the best of both worlds: career opportunities and an education at one of the most respected institutions in the South.

People think of education as book learning; that college is all about going to class and getting good grades. But for me, an education is so much more than that: It's about taking advantage of the opportunities that are available to you.

From my first day at school, I took full advantage of all the on-campus resources. I looked at college as a safety net: I was in a confined atmosphere with ten thousand other students, and it wasn't the whole world yet. Why not try and experiment? Since I knew I wanted to do radio and TV, I found every outlet available to me. I worked at the campus radio station with Cherié Lofton and the program director, Tony Welborne, doing graveyard shifts, even counting down the New Year from the booth, eventually getting my own show on Monday afternoons. I hung out at the on-campus TV station, under the guidance of two Communication Department professors—Gail Wiggins and Nagatha Tonkins—who let me borrow equipment and film segments around school. I built a radio reel. And anytime I could have a microphone in my hand, I held it.

I utilized anything they had at school that might help me gain experience. And to promote myself, I printed up signs in the school's computer lab that read WHO IS TERRENCE J? I taped them up on every door on campus, to the point that when people met me they'd say: "Are you that motherfucker Terrence J? I hate you! The flyer you taped to my door ruined the paint!" Soon, everyone knew my name, even if they had no idea who I was.

Promotion was a lot different back in 2000. Social media was in its infancy; Myspace and Facebook didn't even exist yet. All of the current tools for promoting events and getting your word out hadn't been invented. Instead, it was very simple: If you wanted to promote a party on a college campus, you had to find someone to design flyers and then go pass them out. Promotion was hand to hand, approaching people, and getting in their faces. It's a skill set that's given me an edge to this day. Maybe kids who went to college ten years later than I did are a lot faster on a computer, but in the room, against that same person, I'm an animal. I'm not afraid to put myself on the line and risk failure or embarrassment by approaching someone.

These days, you can go on a social media outlet and follow someone, direct-message them, or "like" them, rather than going up to them in person or giving them a call. It takes some of the courage out of communication; there are fewer stakes involved; and as a result, less sincerity and personal contact. And I often run into young people who tell me they don't know how to talk to their managers, or write a letter in full sentences instead of slang and emoticons. Technology should never overshadow the importance of learning how to communicate directly.

That's why, even though I'm active on social media, I try my best to have real-life interactions as much as I can. I'll pick up the phone or set up a face-to-face meeting. I try not to let technology consume my life. Instead, I try to respect the one-on-one conversation and the genuine connection.

I can definitely trace building my skills in this regard back to North Carolina A&T. Will Smith says there's a difference between skill and talent—talent is something you're born with, but to have skill is to tirelessly work to the best of your ability to hone that talent. Not convinced? In another one of my favorite books, *Outliers*, the author Malcolm Gladwell writes that in order to be great at anything, you need to practice for ten thousand hours. Why was Michael Jordan such a great ballplayer at age seventeen? Because he picked up his first basketball at age six and never put it down. Why was Michael Jackson so incredible? Because he started singing at age five. To be truly great takes years of experience; it has to be an everyday thing in your life, the thing that you eat, breathe, and sleep. This relentless practice is what separates the greats from those who are just good, the Chris Pauls, the Dwyane Wades, and the Carmelo Anthonys from the guy playing ball at your local park.

In college, entertainment and promotion was my breath. Every day of every week, and all weekend, all I was thinking about was *How am I going to get better?* I worked so many free talent shows, spent so many hours in the radio booth, and hosted a million banquets, happy just to hold a microphone night after night. And every single time I did it, I learned something. I learned how to understand crowd energy, stole techniques from other people I watched, and created my on-air persona.

People think of school the wrong way. It's not all about the classroom. School is where you sharpen your blade. It's about the opportunities you get while you're there: doing things by trial and error, playing around, learning your passions in an environment of no risk. I messed up tons of those shows at school, but it was okay. It was school, and everyone else was learning just like me.

I was having a blast at college, but my mom tried to keep me grounded. "It's great that you have a voice," she'd say when I called home to brag about the latest gig I'd hosted. "But at some point you're going to want to use that voice for more than just promoting parties and talking about events and chasing after girls. You're going to want to use it for good."

My junior year of college, I found out what she was talking about. A student named Christopher who lived next door to me in my freshman dorm was shot and killed at a local nightclub. It was a horrible, random act of violence. Gun violence was on the rise in our community, creeping into A&T, and the campus was starting to feel divided. A&T had a long relationship with the civil rights movement. Four A&T students had been the Greensboro Four, the activists responsible for staging one of the first and most influential sit-ins at the start of the civil rights movement. Jesse Jackson had attended college here, too. In that spirit, my friends Travis, Fred, and LaShawn "Quiet" Ray and I decided to organize a Unity March. Our student adviser, Mr. Maltese, helped us organize an event that became a huge success—more than a thousand students marched from the nightclub where Christopher was shot, back to the campus for a rally and candlelight vigil. I gave a speech about the importance of sticking together as a community. I was inspired by what had happened to speak out for an end to violence. For the first time, I understood the power of my voice.

Motivated by this experience, I decided to run for class president, and I was lucky enough to win. My senior year was insane: Now, not only was I doing my radio show and hosting, but I was running a $500,000 operating budget, organizing campus concerts and step shows, learning money management and public speaking, and trying to please my constituency. It was my first experience living in the public life. Oh yeah, and I still had to pass my classes.

On top of everything else, I had joined Omega Psi Phi, one of the most prestigious black fraternities in the country. So, for the last six months of college, I was operating on two or three hours of sleep at most. During the day, I would be in a suit giving speeches in between classes; at night, I would be running through the woods with my fraternity brothers, doing the full military-style training that was part of our pledge process.

There wasn't a single opportunity in college that I missed. I may have been exhausted, but it was one of the most fulfilling times of my life. Every skill that I have today, I honed at A&T. My college years from 2000–2004 really shaped my life.

Tiffany was quiet and still. When I glanced down, I saw that Tyler had fallen asleep in her arms, a bottle still in his mouth. She and I watched him for a while, as peaceful as can be. Finally, Tiffany whispered, "You said your mom never stopped trying to go back and finish her education. Did she ever get her degree?"

She didn't manage to go back to college for a bachelor's degree, but she never stopped trying to find opportunities to expand her education. And watching her helped remind me that I needed to keep learning, too.

A few years after I graduated from college, I was working in New York City, hosting *106 & Park* on BET. I was working hard, but wasn't necessarily taking my job as seriously as I could: I was having a blast, going to parties and premieres, meeting hip-hop artists whose work I loved, and having a lot of fun. Then my mom called to tell me that she'd gone back to school: She'd started taking that contractors' course, and was going to get her certificate. A few months later, I drove down to North Carolina to cheer her on as she graduated. It was a real eye-opener. She was forty years old and still trying to further her education. What was *I* doing to further mine?

At the moment, not very much. Once again Mom showed me a better way through her actions.

When I got back to New York, I took a look at the bigger picture of my life. I wasn't going to be twenty-three years old and hosting *106 & Park* forever. What did I want to be doing when I was forty? I decided that, like my mom, I needed to go back to school.

I'D LET MY PURSUIT of acting fall by the wayside over the years. So I signed up for acting workshops at the famous Lee Strasberg Institute—where the greatest actors, like Al Pacino and James Dean, studied their craft. Maybe I wasn't going out on auditions at the moment, but I needed to use my free time to hone my skills so that when things did happen, I'd be ready. I attended class four hours a day, three days a week—after working my full-time job—for more than two years, eventually earning my full acting certificate.

And I'm still not done. I'll never be. Someday, when I accomplish what I want to do in TV, I'd love to get a master's in communication. The marketplace is always changing, and I'd love to learn more about the digital direction our industry is taking. I'd love to speak Spanish fluently, too. There's always more to learn.

Tyler began to stir. Tiffany stood, carefully trying not to jostle him awake, and smiled wryly. "Too bad they don't offer degrees in diapering and formula," she said. "I'd have a Ph.D. by now."

I laughed. "True, true. But seriously . . . you know what I mean. Don't give up on bettering yourself. You've got way too much future ahead of you to do that."

In Her Own Words: Lisa on the
Importance of Learning

I have an innate need to learn new words. I keep a busted, beat-up dictionary by the chair where I sit every evening. And if I'm watching TV or listening to the radio and hear a word that I don't know, I look it up. It's just my thing—something I love to do.

I'm constantly reading, looking at things, learning. I like to think of reading as "Sailing Toward Knowledge"—that's the meaning of the crest with the picture of the boat that I put in Terrence's books. Knowledge is power. Information helps you harness the world.

Raising Terrence, college was paramount for me. I didn't want any doors to be closed to my kid, that's why by hook or crook Terrence had to finish school. But information and learning isn't just something you get from school; it can come from books you read, people you meet, wherever you can find it. Take the best information you can get from any and all of the smartest minds you know.

Jaime and I call it the Art of Living. It's something you never finish working on—there's always new technology becoming available. New books with new ideas. New complications to life, new circumstances, new things to experience. If you stop learning, you stop growing. As long as we're here and breathing, every day is an opportunity to learn more.

You can learn something from anything and anyone. From a clerk at the grocery store, the busboy at the restaurant, even animals. But we have to be open to it. I'm inquisitive, I ask questions. I listen to the answers. I pay attention to what is around me and what other people are doing, showing, saying. Just observe. Because if you're talking, you can't listen.

Romany Malco Talks About His Mom

*Romany Malco is an actor, Renaissance man, and one of the most
interesting people I know. Originally from Brooklyn, New York,
his breakthrough roles came on the Showtime series* Weeds *and
his hilarious turns in the now classic* The 40-Year-Old Virgin
and Baby Mama. *I met Romany on the set of* Think Like a Man,
*and we have become friends. I talked to him about his mother on
the set of* Think Like a Man Too, *and he told me about how her
fun-loving personality sparked something in him.*

My mom had me at twenty-three, and she was very young and
spirited. When I was growing up, she worked at Columbia University as an accountant. Columbia at the time was one of the top ten
schools in the country, and also one of the most progressive. So her
friends were an incredible mix of people.

I remember when I was six or seven, she used to have all her
friends over, to get ready to go to a party. My mom would be in the
mirror teaching everyone to do the latest dances. I loved her nerve
at that time in her life. She was the ringleader but also the person
who brought all walks of people together, a really culturally diverse
group. You name it, we had it: any nationality, whatever your sexual
preference was, it didn't matter. They were all here with us.

Looking back, this is what people try to portray in movies now, but it was my real life because of my mom. I loved how spirited and inclusive she was. I think it had a lot to do with her West Indian roots.

This transferred into my life, and now I'm the same way. The reality is, the majority of this country is very segregated. And if you're not exposed to things, you sometimes think of them as intimidating; the fact that people are different makes you uncomfortable. I never had that discomfort. I was allowed to experience different things, and that translated into a perspective that seems to be very unlike the perspective of someone who had a standard upbringing in one isolated environment. It made me extremely adventurous. I've been all over the world, and a big part of it was about how adventurous my mom was in her youth.

She was also really encouraging of my interest in entertainment. I grew up with a lot of kids who aspired to be athletes or singers, influential people, attorneys. Most of their moms were saying, "Be realistic and get yourself a job." My mom, for as long as I could remember, was saying, "Hell yes! Here's a talent show, want to get in it?"

That type of encouragement really instills the type of discipline you need to make it life.

My mother, Lisa, has always led by example. Here she is graduating from Springfield Gardens High School in Queens. (1981)

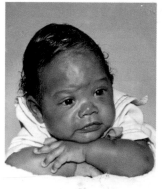

My mom was seventeen years old when I entered the scene. I'm a few months old here in 1982.

My mom and me on the balcony of our apartment in Queens.

The house my mom and Jaime built together in 1997. My mother was determined to make the dream of owning a home a reality for her family.

Our cocker spaniel, Spanky, and me. He was with me for all my big childhood moments. I still miss him. (1996)

My stepfather, Jaime, taught me how to be a man. He's been there for me and my mom every step of the way. (1997)

Me and my Omega Psi Phi line brothers on graduation day in 2004. Going to A&T was an incredible experience for me—I earned a degree and built a support system of friends who have stuck by me. *Bottom, left to right:* (striped shirt) Melvin Heggie, Uche Byrd, Marcellus Foster, Darnell Reid. *Top, left to right:* Jonathan Harmon, Leonardo Mercer, me, Peter Brooks, Mario Lewis.

My mom had always had a plan for my education. She helped me develop a love of reading from an early age—and even made a family crest for each of my books.

My two best friends, fraternity brothers, and business partners: Fred Whitaker and Travis Bond Roseboro.

BET changed my life. I went from running errands to interviewing A-list celebrities. Here are Rocsi and me on the couch with Denzel Washington and Jay-Z. It was unreal. (2007)
© *WireImage/Johnny Nunez*

Rocsi and I share a laugh with the always hilarious Jamie Foxx. (2009)
© *WireImage/Johnny Nunez*

After seven years hosting *106 & Park* with Rocsi it was hard to say good-bye, but it was time for me to take my next step. (2012)

Think Like a Man won the 2013 BET Award for Best Movie. Accepting the award, one year after leaving BET, was one of the most gratifying moments of my life. (2013)
© *Getty Images for BET/Mark Davis*

In 2010, Haiti was struck by a devastating earthquake. Four of my best friends and I went down to help with the relief effort. Here, a woman asked me to hold her baby so that she could carry more supplies home.

The experience I had in Haiti completely changed my perspective on my life and on the world. We raised $10,000 in donations to help provide food and water for the people we encountered.

Hollywood producer Will Packer took a chance on me and helped launch my career as an actor. Here we are on the set of *Think Like a Man Too* in 2013. Kevin Hart is in the background, stealing the scene as always.

My mentor and fraternity brother, Steve Harvey. (Atlanta, 2009)

In November 2012 I joined *E! News* as a coanchor with Giuliana Rancic. I couldn't be happier. E! Entertainment has opened up so many opportunities for me.

The cast of Steve Harvey's *Think Like a Man* is like my second family. Here we are in Vegas on June 13, 2013, on the set of *Think Like a Man Too*.

The coolest part of my job is getting to hang out with incredible people like Brad Pitt. (2012)

I hope to have one of these of my own someday. (85th Annual Academy Awards, 2013)

6

My Mother's Words of Wisdom About Loyalty

*N*ot long after our conversation, Tiffany sent me an email letting me know that she'd bailed on going to Howard. "I couldn't figure out how to do it and get a job and take care of Tyler, especially with Sean refusing to leave New York," she wrote. I felt for her—it was the same dilemma my mom had faced, decades earlier. Things haven't changed that much, it seems—there just aren't that many resources for young, single moms.

Despite her hard call, Tiffany was feeling good. She had found a job working at a small boutique in Brooklyn, owned by an independent fashion designer who had been impressed by the home-sewn dresses that Tiffany was now selling in her Etsy shop. Tiffany's hustle had paid off. The boutique owner took Tiffany under her wing and was mentoring her, teaching her everything she knew about manufacturing clothes. Maybe Tiffany wasn't in college, but she was getting a *kind of education just the same. Her grandmother was even pitching in, after initially refusing—she'd lost her job as a cafeteria worker in a local high school, and while she was unemployed she was watching Tyler for free.*

Meanwhile, I was in the process of moving to Los Angeles. I'd taken a new job as the coanchor for E! News, *alongside Giuliana Rancic. This was a very exciting career move. Even though I was moving to the other side of the country, I'd promised Tiffany that we'd keep in touch. Sometimes she would call when she needed to get something off her chest. Recently, she'd been venting to me about her old high school friends, who had disappeared off to college and looked to be living the carefree life that Tiffany once thought she'd be living, too. They say the fastest way to make God laugh is to tell him how your life will turn out. It is amazing how much can change in a year.*

"Sometimes I read their status updates or see their pictures online and it bums me out," she told me. "They're all about parties and road trips and staying up all night having fun. I can't even remember the last time I went to a party. Of course I love Tyler to death, but sometimes I feel like I'm missing all the fun parts of life. It's like I'm eighteen going on eighty."

"People only post the good stuff online," I told her. "I bet if you went to go visit them you'd see that their lives aren't a highlight reel all the time. They struggle, too. But you'd never know it from their photos."

"Maybe." She brightened. "You know, my girl Christina has been trying to get me to visit her at college. Maybe I'll take Tyler up for the day."

She rang me again a week later, early in the morning. It sounded like she was . . . on a bus?

"I'm headed back to New York," she said. "I visited my girl Christina up in Syracuse. Bad idea."

"Rough night?"

"The worst." Her voice was scratchy. "I let Christina talk me into going out to a party. Her roommate said she'd watch Tyler for me. And it sounded like a good idea, just to get a break, you know? Hang out with people my age for once. Except that Christina and her new friends, all they talk about is boys and the clubs they've been to, and I didn't have anything in common with them anymore so I ended up getting really drunk. And then when we got back to the dorm at three in the morning I found Tyler by himself, crying, in a dirty diaper, and Christina's roommate was nowhere around. And then no one could understand why I was so worked up about it.

"I should never have left Tyler with someone I didn't know. Just to go party. That was just stupid. But mostly I'm pissed at Christina. She couldn't understand why I was so mad at her roommate. She acted like I was making a big deal out of nothing. It's like—she's not even remotely interested in what my life is like now. And she didn't offer to hold Tyler. Not once. I thought we were best friends."

I may not know much about teenage girls, but loyalty—that's universal, and a subject I know a lot about.

I NEVER KNEW I was a Yankee until I moved to North Carolina. When we arrived in Raleigh, in fifth grade, it was a big enough city to feel familiar to me, and yet it was a completely different world. I was an outsider. My whole family was. In North Carolina, if you weren't born there, you will never truly belong. Lots of folks called us Yankees. They still do.

I had always been a good kid in New York City, but ironically, in North Carolina—where we had moved to escape the dangers of the city—I began courting trouble. When we arrived in Raleigh, in 1991, the city was at the very beginning of a long boom that would double the population—from about 200,000 to 400,000—over the next twenty years. Raleigh is one corner of the Research Triangle Park, an economic magnet with top technology firms and big universities. And as the city's economy grew, it lured people from all over—including big cities like Chicago and New York. Big-city troubles started to pop up, too.

By the time I hit junior high, the drug dealers had found my neighborhood. A bad element was starting to take over the schools; if you didn't do what they wanted you to do, they would rough you up. Already, I'd been targeted, for being a "Yankee" and an outsider.

One day, at the swimming pool in our neighborhood, a kid I went to school with dunked me. I dunked him back—maybe a little too hard, but still, typical boy stuff. The next thing you know, he wanted to fight. The lifeguards quickly broke up our little poolside scuffle, but as he was dragged away, the kid yelled one final warning: "When I see you at the bus stop tomorrow, I'm going to shoot you."

I was terrified. It was entirely possible that this kid actually owned a gun—there were kids in my school who did. Maybe he really *would* shoot me as we waited for the school bus tomorrow. That night, I told my mom about the kid's threat. She was horrified.

The next morning, as I readied myself to go face the bus stop, my mom got dressed like a boy, with her hair tucked up under a baseball hat. When I left for the bus stop, she waited until I was almost out of sight, and then silently followed me.

I don't know what my sweet, charming mother thought she was going to be able to do to protect me; she had a steel backbone but it's impossible to imagine her ever getting rough with a kid. When I later asked her what she was thinking, she told that she figured that if someone really was going to pull a gun on me, I better have someone at my back, too. As she said, "As a mom you just do whatever's necessary to make sure that your kid doesn't get hurt."

At the bus stop, I waited nervously for the kid to arrive.

Unbeknownst to me, my mom was also waiting, hidden behind a big tree a few feet back—far enough away that the kids couldn't see her, but close enough that she could jump in if something happened.

When the bus arrived, the kid immediately got off of it, surrounded by his posse. Within a minute, we were in a face-off. I pulled off my jacket, and threw down my bag. "What are you gonna do?" I shouted at the boy.

The kids were trying to egg him on. "Get him!" they cried.

"If you're gonna shoot me, just shoot me!" I said.

Maybe it was because I was acting so fearless, or maybe he was just a scared kid in over his head, too, but he backed down almost immediately. "Forget you, man," he muttered. Before I knew it, he'd slunk off with his posse in tow, and never bothered me again. The gun he'd threatened had never materialized. My mom, invisible behind the trees, breathed a sigh of relief that she wouldn't have to intervene after all.

I never knew that my mom was back there, watching everything— she made sure that she disappeared before any of the kids could see her and start teasing me about being a mama's boy. And yet, I know the story so well that it's as if I actually can see her. Hiding in the trees, all in black, with her hat pulled down low over her head. It wasn't until later, when she told me what she'd done, that I truly understood how ferociously protective she really was. She was willing to do whatever needed to be done to keep me from harm.

I wonder if my bravado that day was because I sensed that she had my back—even though I didn't know she was actually there. I do know that I am incredibly lucky that the kid didn't make good on his threat with a gun. But it is a fact that something inside me was confident enough in her constant care and protection that I felt safe to stand up for myself. I knew that I wasn't alone, and that no matter what, she was there for me. Because of that, I could be brave.

One of the things my mom always likes to say is, "You're only as good as the team that you have behind you." As a kid, facing that bully, I may have only implicitly understood what those words really meant, but as I grew up, that same message—*You're only as good as the team you have behind you*—would come to shape my entire adult life.

It all starts with my family, of course—my first team. We were a tight-knit unit. It was always just the three of us: my mom, Jaime, and me. And we were fiercely loyal to each other. Everything my mom did was about making sure that I had a great life, and that nothing happened to me. Despite having left New York City for "greener pastures," she wasn't going to let her guard down.

As she says, "The experience that the black male has in this country is different from anyone else's, even a black female. I'd seen what happens to young black men. I only had one, and I couldn't mess up. I had to make sure you were physically protected." All you have to do is look at the statistics—African American men are at the top when it comes to murders, incarceration, and drug offenses—to know that she's right. There are just a lot more dangers lurking out there for young black men in America, or all young people in America for that matter. When I went to school, fistfighting was the norm; now, with all of the gun violence prevalent in our society, our youth today have it much worse.

No matter how hard my parents were working, they kept an eagle eye on me. If I had an after-school program, my mom or Jaime picked me up. She knew all my teachers; visited the school regularly to make sure I was getting the education I needed; attended every performance. Even though both my parents worked multiple jobs, I was never a latchkey kid. They arranged their work schedules so that there was always someone home when I got home from school; always a fresh, hot, home-cooked meal for dinner; always someone to help me with homework. She knew every one of my friends by name, kept an eye out for any bad elements. Her focus was always 100 percent on me: She knew that if anyone in this world needed someone at his back, propping him up, it was an African American teenage boy.

Growing up, I was intensely aware of how important our little crew was; how much I could count on my mom and Jaime no matter what happened. I also began to learn how rare it was, so I knew that I had a great gift in that kind of security. And I also came to understand that this kind of fierce loyalty should extend to friendships, too. My mom wasn't much of a socialite—besides Jaime and me her inner circle included just a few people—but those few friends she had were close.

As she put it, "I'd rather have a small group of friends I can count on than a lot of friends that aren't good for anything." Mom took care to surround herself only with people who were moving in the same direction she was. With a small circle, she explained to me, there's never any confusion. Everyone knows their role and works accordingly.

I was inspired, watching her and the way she operated. She helped me understand that I didn't have to be popular; I didn't have to try to be everyone's friend. In life, she showed me, it's more important to keep your team tight, your friendships close, and work with people that have the same goals and vision as you.

To this day, I can look back and see how this advice has shaped my life. Thanks to her inspiration, I built a close network of friends that not only always has my back—just as she did that day in Raleigh—but whose loyalty and support has taken me to where I am today.

It was pretty quiet on the other end. "You still there?" I asked.

"Yeah," said Tiffany. "Tyler's asleep on my lap. But I'm listening. You sound like my grandma, talking about how my friends are bad influences on me. She never liked Christina, said she was 'lacking moral fiber.'"

My mom used to tell me that you are the sum of the people in your inner circle. If you hang around people who aren't motivated and don't want to do anything with themselves, get in trouble, skip class, and have no goals, that's who *you* will become as well. "It's imperative that you surround yourself with the right people," she'd say.

"Surround yourself in mud and you're gonna get dirty." Mom sure had a way with words.

My inner circle? My two best friends, my brothers: Fred Whitaker and Travis Bond Roseboro.

Fred is a quintessential New Yorker: motivated and fast on his feet. He's a general with a soldier's mentality, the guy who gets the job done. He excels at building relationships quickly. He's five feet ten at best, but he's wiry and strong, and he still thinks he's got a shot at going to the NBA. At our age, we all still play basketball, but he *practices*. I think he still believes that he's going to get drafted by the Knicks one day. After all these years in the business, he's met everyone from Rihanna to Denzel Washington, but the only person he's ever tried to take a picture of is NBA coach Pat Reilly.

Travis is more systematic. He's a very diligent, hard worker, and smart as all hell. I love his sense of humor—sarcastic and witty. He's six feet one and two hundred pounds and he's always saying that he's gonna get abs—so far I haven't noticed them. I bet him $10K that he still won't have abs by the time this book comes out. We'll see.

I met Travis my very first day of college. Travis was already working at the local radio station, which was covering the freshman step show that I had managed to talk my way into hosting. As Travis remembers it, "Terrence ran up with the most energy I'd ever seen, talking a million miles an hour. He was eighteen years old with cornrows down his back. I turned to someone and said, 'This is the corniest guy I've ever met.' But Terrence was wired and ready to go. 'Yeah, I'm gonna be on the radio real soon, too.' Then he ran down the hill and hosted the show and then ran back up. 'How'd I do? How'd I do?'"

We were best friends from that day forward. He was the DJ, and I was the mic man—Travis played the music, I did the talking—and soon we started a business. We became a crew, "Team Dolla." At the radio station, there were three different tiers of employees, the highest of which were the afternoon and morning jocks, who were invited to DJ and host all the big events in town. Travis and I were definitely third tier—we came off the bench when needed, so to speak. Our show was on the air from midnight to six A.M. But we still managed to get ourselves booked hosting events—talent shows and parties and such. It wasn't lucrative or glamorous work— usually $200 a pop, shared—but it helped us pay our bills.

We hooked up with Fred a few months later. Our friend Kim Worth told us that she had a friend who was also a communications major and thought we should meet him, because she thought he would be a great asset to our crew. When we first met Fred, we were suspicious: He was super cocky, had New York swagger, and drove a red 1989 BMW hatchback with all the confidence in the world. I don't trust guys who drive red hatchbacks.

"What do you do?" we asked him.

"I work," he said. "Anything that you can't do yourselves, I'll do it."

So we asked him to pass out flyers for a party we were throwing the next day. That afternoon he went to every parking lot on campus and put a flyer on every single car. Within a few hours, everyone at school was talking about the party. Turned out, Fred was a promotional genius. He came back to us later that afternoon and said, "So, do you have more?"

Travis and I just looked at each other. We knew, from that moment on, the three of us would be working together.

But the night of the party, we truly cemented our friendship. After a successful event, we went to get food at a local IHOP, where we ran into a guy Travis had known since kindergarten. This guy had just gotten an NFL contract, and because he was celebrating that night, we'd sent him some free drinks—which somehow offended his sensibilities. He came to our table, showing off for his entourage at the other table, and threw a crumpled-up twenty-dollar bill in my face: "Don't buy me drinks. I don't need your money."

It was clear that there was about to be an altercation, right there in the middle of IHOP. But it wasn't Travis or me who stopped it—it was Fred, a guy we'd known for all of three days, who jumped up and got in this huge football player's face. "This isn't happening. If you even *touch* one of my friends, you will regret it," he said. I'm not sure why—maybe God was looking down that day—but the football player backed down. He could have beat Fred's ass (although I'm sure Fred doesn't think so). He probably could have beaten up all three of us. It was a testament to Fred's loyalty that he was willing to risk it. Travis has never been scared to throw a punch, either. Luckily, we all lived to fight another day.

Travis and I had met with other guys who wanted to work with us, but they only wanted to hang for the fun parts. Nobody else wanted to do the legwork, or to be there when we needed it. Fred was *loyal*; being friends with him for one day was like being his friend for ten years. He had our back, and we were inseparable from that day on.

Later, our friend Lashawn Ray would join us, completing our little unit. Throughout my college years, the four of us were a team, no matter what we did. We were *brothers*. We were never the coolest crew. There were guys we could have hung out with who had better cars, better clothes, better parties. But my boys? We shared a common vision, even if sometimes it just involved hosting a party for enough money to go to the waffle house for dinner. Collectively, we wanted to be successful. We knew we were stronger as a group. Each of us had different strengths. Instead of getting jealous or ripping each other down, we maximized those strengths. Fred was the business guy and promoter; Travis the brains behind the operation; Lashawn was the connector; and me? I'm a good organizer . . . and speaker, of course. We made a strong team. When we worked together, we made things happen.

There was our DJ and hosting business, sure, but that was only the beginning. Because of the senseless shooting of my dorm neighbor, Christopher, I was motivated to run for student body president. But that required a lot of logistics and management experience, which wasn't my strength.

Fortunately my brothers' skills complemented my own, and my crew of misfits became my campaign managers. And when I won the election, I wanted my team around me more than ever. I had tons of harebrained schemes, but I'm only one man. I needed people to call on to execute my vision. I had an amazing executive board, appointed by students, but my boys became my inner circle in the positions I could appoint. Together, we managed a budget of half a million dollars, producing events for the school including concerts, basketball games, and parties. Those days were magical. I'm proud of what we accomplished there, and it only happened because everybody on the team had the same vision, and we all supported each other. Just like my family, loyalty was on the top of everyone's list.

By the time I graduated, I had a second tight-knit crew, too—my line brothers at Omega Psi Phi fraternity.

Growing up as an only child, I always felt that I missed out on a certain kind of brotherhood. And since we moved so much when I was a kid, I never formed a tight crew in junior or high school. So when I hit college and heard about fraternities, I was really intrigued. I wanted to experience that kind of camaraderie and fellowship.

Founded at Howard University in 1911, Omega Psi Phi now has over 750 chapters worldwide. Many accomplished, high-profile black men are members: Shaquille O'Neal, Tom Joyner, Rickey Smiley, Bill Cosby, and Michael Jordan, to name a few. Two of my most influential mentors, Steve Harvey and his business manager Rushion McDonald—who largely inspired me to write this book— are members of the fraternity as well. I spend a lot of time with Steve discussing business and personal goals, and the connection that we have wouldn't be the same if we weren't both Omega men.

Because Travis was a legacy—his father, Big Al, was a member—he knew that he wanted to join the organization. He was always reading books about the Greek system, researching and talking about it; and the more I heard about Omega Psi Phi from him, the more it sparked my interest, too.

When I first arrived at North Carolina A&T in 2000, the Omega Psi Phi fraternity hadn't existed on campus for several years—there had been issues in the past concerning hazing that led to the organization being suspended from campus. But in 2003, the fraternity was eligible to come back, and that first year of their return there was a lot of buzz around their presence. Omega Psi Phi is a very manly organization, very militant in presence, full of dominant personalities. Where other Greek organizations on campus were smooth and debonair, Omega Psi Phi was about power and edginess—but also intelligence. The guys in Omega, in addition to being big guys and football players, were also future doctors, lawyers, and engineers. That impressed me. Plus, they wear signature gold boots and army fatigues: I remember looking at them and thinking, "Wow, they look cool." All the girls on campus flocked around them. I had to join.

But there were other reasons to join, too: the brotherhood aspect, for instance; the fact that both Travis and Fred were pledging; and, finally, the challenge of pledging itself. That appealed to me. It was a killer process, incredibly difficult. I often heard stories of guys who couldn't make it through—tough, six-foot-four football players who just couldn't cut it. I love a good challenge, and this sounded like the ultimate.

I can't tell you about the process of entering Omega Psi Phi, but I can tell you that it was one of the hardest things I'd done in my life thus far, and one of the most gratifying experiences of my adulthood. I learned about manhood, scholarship, perseverance, and uplift—the four cardinal principals of Omega Psi Phi. I came to understand the meaning of sacrifice and commitment. And I built an incredible lifelong bond with my "line brothers" (pledge class) and my Mu Psi (our college's chapter of Omega Psi Phi) brothers after going through some very dramatic experiences. We still attend each other's bachelor parties and weddings; I sleep well knowing that if anything were to happen to me, they'd take care of my family, and vice versa. Our kids all have twelve godfathers.

My line brothers—Dimitri Yates, Donovan Caves, Richard Patterson, Fred Whittaker, Travis Bond Roseboro, Darnell Reid, Billy McEachern, Jerome Butler, Uche Byrd, Tamario Howze, Charles Biney, and Fred Boone—are my support system. As we say, "Mu Psi until the day I die."

Nearly ten years after graduating, Travis and Fred and I still work together every day: Fred is my business manager, and Travis is the head of digital media for our business. The scale of the deals that we do is much larger now, but it's the exact same formula we perfected when we were twenty years old, throwing parties and hosting events at A&T.

The more successful I've become, the more I've come to appreciate my team, which has grown over time. Money changes people. It leads to jealousy, envy, and complications. That's why loyalty is so imperative. Loyalty means that if everything goes away tomorrow, your crew will still be there. Hollywood is jammed with fair-weather friends. When you have a successful album or film, they'll latch on in order to get a piece of your success. But when things don't go so well? Those types of folks are nowhere to be found.

It is vital to surround yourself with the right people. We are all motivated by our collective vision, our collective brotherhood, and our collective loyalty.

When I think of Omega Psi Phi, and all of my close friendships, I can trace these relationships directly back to my mom. *You're only as good as the team you have behind you.* Thanks to my mom's good advice, I have the best team in the world behind me. People who step up and hold me when I need help, people who make me feel incredibly secure. People who directly helped me achieve all the things—joining the fraternity, winning student body president, and becoming a TV host—that ultimately made me the success that I am today.

Just like my mom, hiding in the bushes and watching out for me on that day so long ago, they have my back—no matter what. And I can never thank them enough. I've got their backs, too.

In the background, I could hear Tyler waking up. "We're not there

yet, little man. Still an hour to go," Tiffany murmured. Then, to me—
"Hey—I gotta run, Tyler's waking up and he's gonna be hungry."
"Of course."
She hesitated. "You have my back, right?" she asked.
"Always," I said.
"Just checking."

In Her Own Words: Lisa on Loyalty & Friendship

You are only as successful as the team that you have. No one makes it alone. You have to have support no matter what.

Family is the main team, at the core of everything. When I met Jaime, I thought, "Now I can choose this person to form a team with." Parents are like a tree: If the tree isn't strong, the limbs— the kids—won't be strong. It takes that strong base. At the end of the day it's all about your family: If anything happens, those are the people who have your back.

And friends, too. Anyone will be in your corner when you ride in the limousine; will those people still be there when you have to ride the bus? Terrence's industry, the media, can sometimes be a monster, so you have to be careful whom you're around. When things are going great, people will jump on your coattails, but a lot of people aren't genuine. When something happens, are those same people still going to be in your corner?

When it comes to your friends, you have to ask yourself, does this person have my best interest at heart? If a fight breaks out, is that person gonna jump in and help me out, or is he going to say "I ain't gonna get involved"?

Every life has its peaks and valleys. There are times when you are up, and everything's great; and then—like everything else—there's a dip. You want to have people on your team who are willing to be there for the grind, not just when the magic happens. That's what loyalty is.

Sometimes we can get caught up thinking: This is it; this is all I can do. Then you find someone supportive and loyal who believes in you—your family or your friends. When your team believes in you, it helps you be more than you can be. Because of Terrence and Jaime believing in me, I'm smarter, bolder, and wiser now than I was ten years ago. They make me a better person, stretching and growing. They help me to see what's possible, and encourage me, give me the tools that I need to be successful and believe in myself.

I'm going to be fifty very soon and I'm always thinking about how I can still make them proud of me.

T.I. Talks About His Mom

Clifford Harris, better known as T.I., is an author, actor, record executive, and three-time Grammy Award–winning hip hop artist who has had numerous hit singles, including four that have reached number one on the Billboard Hot 100 *chart.* Billboard *called him the Artist of the 2000s decade. He grew up in Atlanta, and his role in the semibiographical film* ATL *brought him acclaim as an actor. He shared with me how he and his mom didn't always see eye to eye, but their mutual respect and great love has carried them through the good times and the tough.*

For the longest my mom and I did a lot of bumping heads, you know. My ambitions were other than the wishes that she had for me—whether it was my previous experiences in—how do I say?—the pharmaceutical trade, or me putting all of my energy and efforts into the music, and allowing myself to be distracted from my schoolwork. My momma, man, she was always huge on education; she would go on about it. I got grounded a lot, and worse than that.

My momma, she used to fight with my uncles when I was a kid. I would see my momma fighting with grown men: *bim bam bow.* She was younger then, of course, but she was running around handling things like men do.

I think all of that contributed to me being the man I am today—the stubbornness, the confidence, and believing in myself, whether people agree with me or not. A lot of that came from my experiences with her. Her being real, on her own and independent, and not really bending or conforming to whatever it was that other women did when they were in relationships with men.

My mom only had one boyfriend after my dad, and I was always the man in the house. No one ever came in the house and presented himself as a second dad. It was always me and her. Anything we needed between the two of us, we got. That bond, it introduced me to my young adulthood with a sense of loyalty and an idea of what it takes to be a provider, to really be a boss and call your own shots. And how to rest on your own abilities.

My mom is my partner. Come hell or high water, low times or the highest times. She is always going to be in support of me, and we of each other. If we gonna chastise each other, it'll be in private, never in public.

We need to appreciate our moms more; without you there could not be us. We may not take enough time—more than the third weekend in May—to stop and say we appreciate you and hold you in high regard and respect you. But whatever we accomplish it's because of y'all.

7

My Mother's Words of Wisdom About Dreams & Perseverance

*A*nd here things had been going so well. Less than a month after we last spoke, Tiffany's out of a job. The boutique where she was working had to close up shop—the recession finally got to them—and she was let go along with everyone else. When she called me up recently, she was devastated.

"I went around and applied at every clothing store and fashion company I could find. I even tried to get a job answering the customer service line at Macy's. But no one is hiring. There are a million other girls who want the same job I want, and most of them don't have to worry about flex hours or day care, either."

"I thought your grandma offered to watch Tyler."

"Yeah, that's another thing—she says she can't do it anymore, it's too hard on her to chase Tyler around now that he's crawling. Plus, she's got to go out and look for her own job."

"Hey, you okay?" I asked.

"At least I'm getting to spend more time with Tyler. And Sean's been showing up with a lot more money than he usually does, so we're not hurting too bad."

"Sean got a job?"

She mumbled her response. "Not that I know of."

Uh-oh. I didn't want to ask where the money was coming from, and I'm pretty sure she wouldn't want to tell me anyway. I encouraged her to keep looking for work—there had to be a job in the fashion industry for her, somewhere. She just had to keep her eyes on the prize.

But Tiffany wasn't hearing me. "Maybe it was all a stupid idea anyway—making clothes. It's like a fantasy job, not a real job. It's not practical."

"If that's what you love, it's not a fantasy."

Tiffany snorted. "Practical is a nine-to-five job with health insurance. Practical is not trying to sell silk dresses in the middle of a recession."

"You'll never know if you don't try."

"Maybe I'm not cut out for fashion, anyway."

I didn't know what to tell her. And then I realized that I'd never told her about how I got my job at 106 & Park, *the job that truly launched my career. It's a great story about how perseverance pays off. My mom firmly believed that you should never give up on your dream, and in my case, her advice was spot on.*

. . . . .

ONE OF MY MOM's favorite sayings is "the harder you work, the luckier you'll get." Growing up, she must have said this to me a hundred times, a thousand times. If you wake up every morning, dreaming about the thing that you want, and work every day to make it a reality, doors will open and things will happen.

When I was ten years old, my mom encouraged me to make a vision board of the things that I wanted most from life. You've probably seen these—a vision board is basically a bulletin board with inspiring images pinned on it, clippings and photos and pages from magazines to help you focus on the things that you want to achieve. I still remember the vision board I created that year. On it, I pinned a photograph of a big house on a hill. An ad for a shiny new red Ferrari. And images, torn from magazines, of the three people I admired most at the time: Michael Jordan, Oprah, and Will Smith.

I never grew tall enough to play basketball—not much I could do about that—but my other two heroes remained a source of inspiration and aspiration all through the years. No matter which direction I strayed in my interests, I always came back to these two. One was a legendary broadcaster, TV host, and entrepreneur. The other is one of our most charismatic actors and producers. The older I grew, the more I came to recognize that these were the areas where my true passions lay.

It's not a surprise that I grew up with a love for acting and entertainment. My stepdad is a huge film buff. As I grew up, Jaime would sit me down in front of old Alfred Hitchcock films and pepper me with questions as we watched: What did I like about the film? What was the director doing? What did I think about that actor? We'd spend hours on the couch, watching old Hollywood classics with Audrey Hepburn, Gregory Peck, and James Dean, as well as more recent action films starring Robert De Niro and Al Pacino (my mom wasn't thrilled about the latter—she'd cover my eyes, give me the earmuffs when anyone swore—but Jaime would let me watch anyway). Jaime liked to tell me stories about how he grew up watching Marlon Brando, explain how the images that you consume can end up shaping your life. I didn't realize it at the time, but he was teaching me an appreciation for storytelling.

Meanwhile, my mom was a big media person. She was always watching the news, staying up to date on current events, music, entertainment, and fashion. She also understood the importance of presentation. She constantly reminded me to stand up straight, look people in the eyes, shake hands, speak to the room, enunciate, be nice to people. From her, I inherited a fascination with popular culture and an appreciation for the power of good communication.

Without being aware of it, my mom and my stepdad were

grooming me for my eventual double career: as an actor and TV host. Before I'd even made it to high school, I was pinning new photos to my inspiration board and spending hours at the library (these were the days before Wikipedia) doing research on icons like Eddie Murphy and Denzel Washington, Dick Clark and Jay Leno.

The good news was that I didn't just have an interest being in front of an audience, I had the personality for it, too. In high school, I was a huge class clown, constantly cracking wise for anyone who would listen. One of my teachers eventually pulled me aside and said, "You can make people laugh—you have a big mouth. Just make sure that that big mouth puts you in front of a check, and not behind bars."

When I told my mom what my teacher had said, she laughed. But she also agreed, "She's right." It was easy to just goof around and be a class clown, but if I really wanted to work in entertainment—if I wanted to put my big mouth to work for me—I had to be prepared to do the hard work that it would take to get there. It wasn't enough to just have some photographs of actors pinned on a bulletin board.

My mom had already shown me how this was done. Growing up, I often thought about the day that she packed all of our family's belongings into a U-Haul and drove us south from New York City to North Carolina. I remember that before we got in the car, I told her that I didn't want to go. North Carolina was too far from my friends, I grumbled; too far from everything. Why did we have to move?

My mom crouched down next to me: "When you have a vision, you have to see it through, no matter how far you have to go to get it," she said.

Throughout my life, these words would echo back to me. That day, as we began the long drive south to North Carolina, my mom's vision was to raise me in a place that was safe, in a house that she had paid for herself, with a dog for me to play with. Every decision she made with her life in the years to come was about working toward her personal dream board, no matter how distant or challenging it seemed. And by the time I got to high school, she'd achieved all of those dreams.

As for me and my dream of being an actor and entertainment news host? It never would have happened if my mom hadn't pushed me in the right direction, at just the right moment.

FLASH FORWARD TO THE summer of 2005. Less than a year out of college, I was an account executive at NASCAR, working in their diversity department and living in Daytona Beach, Florida. It was a great job; a job with a lot of potential upside; a job with stability, benefits, and great coworkers. I loved it there.

But it wasn't my passion.

The truth was, at just twenty-three years old, I had already given up on my dream of acting and working as a host. At the very last minute, after pursuing my vision all through college—taking acting classes, hosting my radio show, running events for my college and fraternity—I had chickened out. I had listened to teachers who told me that you couldn't be a host and an actor at the same time: "It just doesn't make sense," they'd said. I had listened to the people who told me that I shouldn't try to pursue my dreams right after I graduated from college: "You can't be an actor: You live in North Carolina, not Hollywood." "You're not Will Smith." "You need a real nine-to-five job that will make payments to your 401k." You're not smart enough, fast enough, handsome enough to do the things you want to do, they'd said; and I had listened.

Worst of all, I had listened to my own fears.

The summer after I graduated from college, I had flown out to Los Angeles to give acting a real Hollywood try. I spent three weeks there going to auditions nonstop. *X-Men, Superman, Dreamgirls, Pirates of the Caribbean, Fast & Furious, the Pursuit of Happyness, Mission: Impossible*—if it was a movie with an open casting call, I was the first one in line, script in hand. I was convinced that this was the first step toward turning my vision into a reality. I thought I was en route to being a star.

Instead, I got *slammed*. Among the things I heard about myself: "You're too skinny and too young." "We're looking for a guy who is more built than you." "We don't think we're going African American for this role." "You're too urban." And my favorite: "You suck."

"Don't quit your day job, kid," a casting director told me.

So I didn't.

During my sophomore year of college, one of my professors told me about NASCAR's diversity internship program. NASCAR wanted to bring more racial diversity to the sport of racecar driving—from the drivers themselves to corporate executives and employees. I was intrigued and, with the help of my professor, ended up winning a summer internship at NASCAR's Los Angeles office, in their entertainment department.

It was a great internship—so great that I ended up going back the following two summers. At NASCAR, I learned more about business than I had in my whole life thus far: from how to write a business letter, to how to solicit talent to perform at races, to how to behave when you're on the phone with the highest muckety-mucks at a record label. I solicited performers like Mariah Carey, Jamie Foxx, and Jennifer Hudson, inviting them to races, to sing the national anthem, or to become a grand marshal.

When I returned to North Carolina after auditioning in Los Angeles that summer of 2005, I felt utterly defeated. I let the bad reviews from the Hollywood casting agents and the discouraging words of my teachers convince me that I wasn't cut out for entertainment after all. So when NASCAR called and offered me a

full-time job at their headquarters in Daytona Beach, I decided to take it. "I'm over acting," I told myself. "That dream is done."

Every morning for almost a year, I got up and went to my NASCAR job and told myself that I was happy. And it *was* an amazing job. I was now running the diversity internship program that I had previously interned for. I was going around the country, speaking with young African American and Hispanic kids about opportunities at NASCAR. I was twenty-two years old and was already a gold medallion member of Delta Airlines. I was sitting in business meetings, watching multimillion-dollar deals go down; learning all about licensing, branding, networking. And it was exciting to be breaking new ground for NASCAR. Often, I was the only black kid in the building, in the meeting, getting the pit tour, and that's a powerful position to be in.

But outside of work, I was miserable. I was dirt poor, still paying off a mountain of debt from my college education. I lived in a tiny, barely furnished one-bedroom apartment. I couldn't even afford a TV. (Seriously—I went a whole year with no TV!) With one exception—my college buddy Travis, who was also working with me at NASCAR—all my friends lived far away. Even my girlfriend lived in a different state, and we often went months without seeing each other. I was lonely, broke, and bored.

All I had were books. Instead of going home after work, I would go to the local Barnes & Noble and read. I had rediscovered that love

for the written word that my mom had instilled within me. *Good to Great, The Celestine Prophecy, Rich Dad, Poor Dad, Who Moved My Cheese*—these were books that would end up defining my adult years. And of course, *The Alchemist*.

Almost a year passed this way. Then one day I got a call from Fred. Despite the entertainment industry aspirations Travis and Fred and I had shared in college, now *none* of us was pursuing our true passion. We'd all listened to the same advice, and gotten "real" jobs after graduating. Travis was in Florida, working with me at NASCAR; Fred was working construction in New York City, a job he hated. But as much as we pretended we'd left all that behind, the truth was that we all missed it terribly—life in the spotlight, throwing fun parties, great social lives. We all knew we weren't as happy as we'd been in college, but we rarely talked about the fact that we weren't pursuing our dreams anymore.

On this day, though, Fred surprised me by bringing it up directly. "Hey, man, I know you like NASCAR and all, but what's up with the hosting and acting?"

I was surprised to hear him mention this. "Yeah, I'm over that," I said, defensively.

"That's too bad," he said. "Because BET is hunting for new talent. They're doing open casting calls in Atlanta, Houston, L.A., and New York. The New York one is in a few days. You should come audition."

For a second, my pulse began to race. An image of myself standing in front of a camera flashed through my mind. But I took a breath and played it cool. "Nah, I'm not gonna do any auditions," I said, slowly. "Look—I have a job, a *good* job, and a life plan. If I stick it out at this job I could make it to a director, or a vice president. Hell, I could be the *president* of this company someday. I shouldn't be playing with acting. I already tried that once, I don't need to go down that road again."

"Nah, come on up!" he kept insisting.

When I hung up the phone, I sat there for a long time, thinking. I was tempted to book the next flight to New York. But I remembered all the discouraging words I'd heard when I went out to Los Angeles the previous summer; I remembered all the professors who said that acting was a pipe dream, but a stable job with a 401(k) was a reality. I was listening to the fear, and it was screaming.

And then I picked up the phone again and called my mom.

She heard me out, and then was quiet for a long time. Finally, instead of telling me what to do, she asked me a simple question: "When you wake up every morning, is your heart completely in what you're doing?"

Her question stopped me cold. "I love what I'm doing," I began. And then the truth spilled out of me. "But honestly, I feel like I'm missing something. When I see a Will Smith movie I'm still inspired to be like him. I still want that."

"You're young, Terrence," my mom replied. "You have the opportunity now to follow your dreams. It's important to do it. Do it while you can."

When we got off the phone, I sat there for a long time. I looked up the price of a plane ticket to New York: $700. My bank account balance was $924. Making this risky trip would completely wipe out my savings, a crazy splurge for someone who couldn't even afford a TV. And then I thought back to the day that my family moved down to North Carolina, and my mom's words before we got in the car: *When you have a vision, you have to see it through, no matter how far you have to go to get it.*

Then I picked up the phone and called Fred. "You know what?" I said when he answered the phone. "I'm coming to New York."

"Oh, I've read this story!" Tiffany exclaimed. "This is how you got the job at 106 and Park, right? You went and auditioned twice and . . ." She started to recite my own story back to me; the girl had read her Wikipedia entries, clearly.

"Yes, but I've never told anyone the full details of how it all went down. It's not on the Internet, trust me. It's a long story, but it's a good one."

The line outside the BET headquarters on that June morning must have been two thousand people long. It stretched all the way around 57th Street, circling the building. Fred dropped me off at the break of dawn, where I met my college friend Lashawn Ray, who was also auditioning. But apparently we were already late, because we were near the back of the line.

We stood in that line for five hours, with nothing to do but grow more and more nervous. I was starving, having only eaten a soggy turkey, bacon, and egg sandwich from the deli on 57th Street and 10th Avenue. My feet were killing me. Before I got on the plane, I had called in sick to NASCAR, lying to my boss that I had some sort of stomach flu. Standing there, feeling worse by the minute, I remembered what my mom liked to say: "If you tell people you're sick, you're gonna get sick."

We kept getting closer to the front of the line. We made it into the building, and went through security, then we were walking through the BET offices. A BET employee handed me a nametag to wear around my neck. I saw Big Tigger, one of my idols, walking down the hall.

"I can't believe I'm here," I thought.

And then, finally, we were in the casting room—a big, intimidating studio with photographs of broadcasters on the wall. As I walked in, a casting assistant handed me a single piece of paper with some words on it. This was the script that I was supposed to read:

"Hey, what's up? I'm [say your name] and it's an amazing day here in NYC. Up next is the number five video of the day, the new joint from Jay Z, right here on BET."

I had about ten seconds to read and digest this. And then I

stepped in front of a table of casting agents, who sat studying me. I looked down at the page and back up at them. I could barely absorb the words of the script: I was too anxious, hungry, and overwhelmed.

I bombed.

After I finished stumbling through the lines, a casting agent ushered me up to the table where they all sat. He smiled and put a red mark on the piece of paper I was holding. And then an assistant took me by the arm and walked me toward a door. "Okay, just go through this door," she said, nicely. For a minute, I didn't know where she was taking me. Were they overlooking the way I'd flubbed my lines? Did they like me anyway?

The door opened directly out into the traffic on Tenth Avenue. I'd been ejected. And just like that, my dream was crushed again. I'd never been so depressed in my life.

When Fred picked me up, I showed him the paper with the red mark and shook my head.

"Damn, dog," he said.

The sun was setting. I'd spent the whole day standing in line at BET, and now there wasn't even enough time to grab dinner before my flight back to Daytona Beach. "Just take me to the airport," I said. "I gotta get back to Florida. I can't afford to get fired."

As we drove back across the Brooklyn Bridge, I texted my mom a quick message: *I didn't make it.*

A few minutes later, my phone chimed with a text message back from my mother. *Just don't give up. If they already cut you once, what's the worst they're going to do if you keep on going?*

I read this out loud to Fred and laughed. "Well, they could cut me again," I muttered.

Fred said nothing, sitting behind the wheel. We sat, idling, in New York rush-hour traffic. My day had finally caught up with me: I was exhausted. Before I knew it, I was asleep.

When I woke up, it was dark out. I looked out the passenger window, and was disoriented. It looked like we were in . . . Philadelphia? I glanced at the clock—three hours had passed. We *were* in Philadelphia.

I looked over at Fred. "What are you doing?"

Fred shrugged. "Your mom is never wrong. We might as well keep going."

"What do you mean?"

"Auditions in Atlanta are tomorrow morning. Let's just go."

"You're nuts."

Fred just smiled.

It *was* nuts. But sitting there in Fred's green Nissan Maxima, I was suddenly filled with so much energy and support, coming from my mom and from my friends. They believed in me. I wanted to believe in myself as much as they did. I wanted to share my mom's determination to make my vision a reality.

I looked down at the audition script with the red check mark on it, crumpled on the floor of the car. "Hell. Why not?"

I texted my mom: *Think we are going to try to make audition in Atlanta.*

A few minutes, a text came back: *That's my Terrence.*

But Philadelphia to Atlanta is a twelve-hour drive. It was already eleven o'clock at night. Judging by the crowds in New York City, we needed to be there in Atlanta by six in the morning in order to guarantee a spot in the line. There was no way we were going to make it. But we were unstoppable. En route, I called Jocelynn Jacobs, one of my best friends from college, who had moved to Atlanta. She lived down the road from where the auditions were taking place, at Club 112 on Peachtree Street. I woke her up at two A.M. and asked her to do something I'm not sure I would have done myself. The mission: I needed her to go down to the audition, register in my name, and stand in line until we got there. Maybe she thought I was crazy, but she always had my back: "Of course I'll do it, but I have to be at work by nine-thirty." I thanked her a million times and got off the phone.

I started calling everyone I knew in Atlanta. I needed someone to take the second shift when Jocelynn left for work. After I exhausted all of my local options, I realized I had only one person left I could call. I dialed Travis to ask the unthinkable.

He picked up after my second call. He sounded groggy; obviously I had woken him up as well. I got right to it as he tried to make sense of my outlandish request. "Okay, so let me get this straight. You just flew to New York, auditioned, and got cut. And now you're on your way to Atlanta and you want me to drive up there from Daytona in the middle of the night to swap spots with Jocelynn and wait in line until you arrive?"

Long pause. Reluctantly, I said, "Yep, that pretty much sums it up."

Another long pause. And then, in typical Trav manner, he said, "Okay, cool. But please note, you owe me for this one. And I'm taking your car. I'll put gas in it and meet you there."

I'm not sure what I did in my last life, but I'm damn sure lucky to have my crew.

We drove straight through the night, stopping only for gas and to wash our faces in a public restroom. We ate service station turkey sandwiches and Doritos. While Fred drove, I read the script on that piece of paper over and over, trying to come up with new ways to deliver the lines. By the time we were halfway there, I had them down cold. By seven A.M., I was getting text messages from Jocelynn: "The line is out of control." I made a quick phone call to my office in Daytona Beach, calling in sick for the second day in a row.

We finally arrived in Atlanta, unshowered and delirious with exhaustion, at around noon. Travis and Jocelynn (who skipped work to wait for us) had already been in line for nine hours. Yes, my friends waited in line for me for nine hours. We walked up and down the audition line, which stretched all the way down Peachtree Street, looking for our friends. There were thousands of people waiting outside—even more than in New York City—but Travis and Jocelynn were nowhere to be seen. Finally, we texted them and discovered that they'd gotten there so early that they had already made it inside the building. Praise be!

Tiffany jumped in. "Wow, I can't believe your friends actually did that for you. I wish I had people like that in my corner."

"Like I told you last time—you're only as good as the team you have behind you. That day, I had an amazing team. I still do."

In any case, Fred and I stood there for a minute, trying to figure out how to get inside the club to meet them. Just as we were about to duck under a rail, a giant security guard began to shout at the crowd: "Everybody, go home. We've already handed out a thousand nametags, and that's gonna be it. So if you don't have one, you need to leave. No one gets inside the building unless they already have a nametag."

Fred and I looked at each other as the disappointed crowd began to dissipate. I couldn't believe it had come to this. Somewhere inside the building, Travis and Jocelynn were still standing in line for me, but there was no way to get to them. We'd driven all night long, traveling the entire eastern seaboard, just to find out that it was over?

And then I glanced down at my chest and had an epiphany. I

hadn't had time to change since the audition yesterday afternoon. I was still wearing my dirty clothes. I was still holding the crumpled script with the red check on it. *And I was still wearing my damn nametag.*

Quickly, I walked toward the security guard. I flashed a smile and flashed the nametag—praying that he wouldn't notice that it was from the New York, not the Atlanta, audition—and said, "Sir, I'm so sorry—I was just inside doing my audition and I left my phone in there. Can I go back in and get it?"

He nodded. "Hurry up."

And just like that, I was back in the game.

This time, walking in the door to the audition, I had a completely new sense of confidence. Unlike everyone else in that line, I *knew* what was going to happen when I got in the room. I already had the script: I knew it by heart. I was prepared. I had the motivation of all these good people in my corner, supporting me—my mom, Fred, Travis, Jocelynn. And most important, I had my mom's words in my head: *What's the worst thing they can do to you?* I had no more fear. Once the fear was out of my system, I had nothing left to lose.

This time, I nailed it.

This time, when I finished my reading, the guy smiled at me and said, "That was great." This time, when they sent me to the next door, there was a green check on my script. This time, instead of opening out onto the street, the door opened into another room and another group of casting agents.

I went through three auditions in quick succession, each time getting moved along to the next, delivering the script in front of casting agents and executives and video cameras, until I finally stood in front of BET executive VP Stephen Hill.

After I did my reading, he stood and came over to shake my hand. "Oh my God, you're really good," he said. "The best of the tour so far." He leaned in to read my nametag, and stopped. "Hey, does that say New York City?"

I looked him straight in the eye, remembering that I had nothing left to lose. "Yes, sir," I said. "I just drove down from New York City, where I was cut from the audition. I haven't had a shower or a meal in seventy-two hours, and honestly, I have to go to the bathroom as soon as possible. But there's nothing I want more than an opportunity to work for your company, and if you give me a shot I won't let you down. If you don't give it to me now, you'll see me in Houston. If you don't give it to me there, you'll see me in Chicago. And then in L.A. You're going to see me until you give me the job."

Hill laughed. "How about that," he said. Then he shook my hand again as I was ushered out the door. There was no one left to see. The audition process was over.

I left the club not really knowing what had just happened. Had I just been cut again? It sure felt like I had. But this time I didn't feel like such a failure. I was proud I'd made it to the third round; that was an accomplishment in itself. I'd taken my mom's words to heart and truly seen this through. If this was it, so be it. At least I could say I'd tried my hardest.

Travis and I drove back to Daytona Beach that night; Fred headed back to New York City. The closer I got to home, the worse I felt. Frustration began to set in as I absorbed the futility of the last two days. How many more times would I have to try and fail? I had already learned my lesson once by going to Los Angeles and failing as an actor, and then I went to New York and failed with BET, and then I went to Atlanta and failed again. This had to be the end of the line. Plus, I was just exhausted.

Finally, I called my mom and told her what had happened.

"Don't worry," she said. "Remember what I always tell you—the harder you work at this the luckier you'll get. Never give up. Good things are going to happen to you."

I sighed, growing frustrated. "Mom, I just spent my entire life savings on a plane ticket to New York City and got cut. I drove to Atlanta and embarrassed myself and it amounted to nothing. What else do you want from me?"

She wouldn't back down. "God always has a plan. When it's your time, it's your time."

Back in Daytona Beach, I looked at my inspiration wall for a long time. And then I began to tear up. It takes a lot to make me cry, but I was definitely on the verge. The dream was over, for real this time. I reached up, tore the inspiration board down, and trashed it.

The next three days at work were empty and dispiriting. As much as I loved my job at NASCAR, the fact that I had been so close to my dream made it harder than ever to feel satisfied with my life in Daytona Beach. I was so depressed that I literally got sick—headaches, upset stomach, fever. It served me right for calling in sick the week before.

Finally, on a random Tuesday afternoon, my phone rang. When I answered it, I heard a strange woman's voice. "This is Connie Orlando, from BET, looking for Terrence Jenkins?"

I thought someone had sent a friend to play a trick on me. "Very funny. Shut the hell up."

The lady spoke again, in a more serious tone, and I could tell she was for real. "This is Terrence?"

I thought I was going to have a heart attack. "That's me," I said apologetically, squeaking with nervousness.

"We're looking at your footage from the audition, and we're really excited about you," she said. "You're now a finalist for the new faces search here at BET, and we'd like you to fly up to New York City."

For a second, I almost didn't believe it. Was this a practical joke? I felt like I was flying. *It wasn't over yet!*

The first person I called was my mom. "I told you the opportunity would come," she said, proudly. "Now it's time to show and prove."

I flew up to New York a few weeks later, calling in sick at NASCAR yet again. There, I joined nine other people from across the country for a weeklong competition. I told myself I wasn't making friends—these people were vying for the same job I wanted, after all—but I still couldn't help but liking some of the people I met—including Alesha Renee and Lamorne Morris, who would later become my coworkers and buddies. All week long, the ten of us went through a series of hosting and reporting challenges. At night we all stayed at the Hudson Hotel, but during the day, they sat us all in a small conference room and filmed us, reality-show style, while cameras followed our every move. It felt like being hazed. The whole time, we had no idea how many people they were going to pick—one of us? Four? None?

The person who really stood out to me that week was Rocsi Diaz. From the jump, I knew Rocsi was special. Out of everybody there, she had the most experience, and I was impressed with her work ethic. Over the next seven years, she would become one of my best friends.

Tiffany started giggling, and gave me the look that I get all the time when Rocsi is mentioned. She laughed and said, "Friends, huh?"

Just to set the record straight, after working with Rocsi for all those years, I can say with all honesty that we never dated or had a relationship. What I will say is that we are the exact same age, started at the exact same time, and went through a lot of life experiences together, from dating people to issues with the press to moving on to the next stage in our careers. Through the good times and bad, I'm just thankful that I had a partner that I could lick my wounds with at the end of the day. Although we never dated, she's one of my best friends and we share a deep relationship that I'm very appreciative of. But I did see her half-naked in her dressing room one day, and I'm glad I have such a hot best friend.

But back to the story . . .

Meanwhile, my bosses down in Florida were growing frustrated with my continued absence. A few days into my stay in New York, I got an email from my boss: "We really need to talk when you come back." I hated lying to NASCAR; I knew I was on thin ice. If I didn't get picked, I really needed my job back. Every night, lying in my bed, I'd toss and turn and wonder if I was making the right decision, gambling my future career on something that might not work out.

At the end of the week, on a live broadcast, BET announced the results of the competition. Five of us were brought onstage in the main BET studio. In front of live cameras, we were given feedback on our performances by two of the top BET execs at the time, Reggie Hudlin and Byron Philips, as well as Stephen Hill. When they got to me, they just said: "We don't have a lot of feedback for you—you're going to be a star." It took a minute to even register what they meant—that I had just been chosen as a New Face. Just like that, my life changed forever.

But just because a door opens for you, that doesn't mean your life is going to magically change overnight. People think that as soon as you get hired for a new job, make it to the NBA, or get picked for a reality show, everything is going to be great. You're done! But that's not what happens. Instead, this is when the hard work starts, and the training begins.

For me, the struggle was far from over.

As it turned out, I wasn't being offered a job at BET. Being a New Face didn't mean anything concrete. They weren't offering me money, a contract, or any kind of a regular gig. In a nutshell, the network needed new correspondents and was offering work on a "pay to play" basis: If I did an on-air assignment, they'd pay me for it, but there was no consistent work to keep the lights on. And what were those assignments going to be? It wasn't clear. The "opportunity" was ambiguous at best.

The only thing that *was* crystal clear to me was that there was a chance to do some on-air work for BET—but I needed to be in New York City, near the headquarters, to make it happen.

Racing back to Daytona Beach one last time, I called my mom. "On the one hand, I have this amazing job with real growth possibilities at one of the biggest companies in the world. They've nurtured me and are offering me stability and a 401k and respect in the business world. On the other hand, I have this pipe dream. I don't know what it means, what it looks like, or what the money is like."

I could have predicted what my mom was going to say. "Follow your heart at all times," she advised me. "Sleep on it. Think about it. Don't do anything because you are looking for other people's admiration, or for money, or for respect. Do it because it's what you're passionate about. Do what makes you happy when you wake up in the morning. Do what your heart tells you to do. And you know that, no matter what that may be, I'll support you."

To be honest, though, I knew exactly what I was going to do from the moment I stepped in front of the camera at BET. I walked back into NASCAR that week and quit my day job. It was one of the most nerve-wracking experiences of my life, but surprisingly, they were wonderful about it—"You always have a place with us at NASCAR. Go follow your dreams." It was the warmest good-bye, and reaffirmed to me that I was on the right path—I support and love NASCAR to this day.

By the end of the month, I was back in New York City. I'd blown all my money on that initial flight to New York and breaking my lease in Florida, and had no guaranteed income from BET: I was dead broke. Thank God for Fred's whole family—his mom, Miss Cynthia, let me sleep on a couch in her basement on Long Island. His grandmother Gussie used to make me chocolate cake that I could die for. Everybody in his entire family, from his aunts and uncles to nieces and nephews, supported me through that time, and I am forever grateful.

I decided that being named a New Face at BET was the equivalent of the door being cracked open. Now it was up to me to kick the door down. I behaved as if I had a full-time job at BET. Every morning, I would get dressed and go down to the studio to see if there was any work I could do, any assignment I might be able to jump on. It was the hustle, Lisa Jenkins Gonzalez style.

Some days, especially in the beginning, I spent most of my time just sitting in the lobby. I'd brainstorm segments to produce and pitch them to any producer who walked by. I introduced myself to the directors of photography and the camera guys, to everybody, from Rick Grimes (the executive producer) to Debra Lee (the CEO) herself. I ingratiated myself to Big Tigger, the legendary host of BET's *Rap City,* and essentially became his intern. I'd run and buy his sneakers for him, open for him at the club, and assist him with any errands he needed done, and in return he taught me the ins and outs of hosting. He was my first television mentor.

I jumped at any opportunity to work, no matter how humbling, and assignments eventually began to float in my direction. Every few weeks, the show's producers would call me up: "Ludacris has a record release party." "The host of our countdown show is sick and we need someone to fill in today." Whatever it was, I'd do it. Whenever BET needed someone to cover a fashion show, a red carpet event, a movie premiere, I was there: the guy standing out in the rain, begging celebrities for a sound byte, working his butt off for a shot at the big time.

There were definitely moments when I wondered what the hell I was doing. Two years out of college, my friends from school were getting jobs as engineers or at law firms, growing real success. I, meanwhile, was living in a kind of hell, sleeping on couches and eating my friend's mom's Hamburger Helper. My parents would send money to pay for my metro pass, but they'd already given me so much—my college tuition, my car—that I felt like I'd tapped them dry. I wanted to do this on my own.

And yet—every day, I woke up knowing that I was finally doing what I truly wanted to do. I was learning, getting closer to my dream. As I'd read in *The Alchemist*—this was my personal legend, and I was going to see it to the very end.

The story has a happy ending, of course. After seven months of being what was probably the most persistently visible New Face and unpaid coffee fetcher in BET history, I got a phone call from Stephen Hill. Rocsi was conferenced in with us. "How are you enjoying your time with us?" he asked.

"It's been a lot of fun," I said honestly. Rocsi answered similarly.

"Well, you've shown real dedication and persistence," he said. "It may not have been obvious to you, but we've been grooming you this whole time. And we want you to host *106 and Park*."

It turned out that Big Tigger, who had taken over from AJ and Free, was moving to Washington, D.C., for a huge radio contract, so BET needed two new hosts for its flagship music show. Rocsi was being tapped for the female host and I—Terrence J, this skinny kid from North Carolina—was going to be the male host.

It was one of the happiest moments of my life, so far. I was overwhelmed with joy—I'd taken a leap, and it had paid off. In spades: The contract I was offered was more than I would have made in three years at my old job at NASCAR.

I went on to host *106 & Park* for the next seven years, experiencing some of the highest ratings in the show's history. I interviewed Barack Obama, Madonna, Jamie Foxx, Will Farrell, and—yes, even my personal idol—Will Smith. I leveraged my growing profile on *106 & Park* into an acting career, starring in box office blockbusters like *Think Like a Man*. And finally, I wound up following in the footsteps of Ryan Seacrest, filling his coanchor spot alongside Giuliana Rancic on *E! News*. And I'm just getting started.

The lessons my mom has taught me over the years paid off, big time. She was right about so many things, but especially these three:

1. Surround yourself with positive people. If I didn't have positive people encouraging me, I would have given up.
2. The harder you work, the luckier you become. Doors opened to me because I just kept banging on them.

3. Never, ever, *ever* give up. There's nothing to lose if you keep
   trying. As my mom had put it, the day of that first audition,
   "If they cut you once, what can they do to you now?" That's
   now my motto in life. It all starts, and ends, with that.

I often think about that epic drive from New York City to Atlanta, back in 2005. Everything in my current life seemed to start
that day. But looking back even further, I think of the drive that my
mom made from New York City to North Carolina, fourteen years
earlier. *That* was my real start. "Baby," she'd told me. "I have big
dreams for you, and those dreams start in North Carolina. I have to
follow them. I don't want you to give up on me."

I never gave up on her, and she never gave up on me. And now
we are both living our dreams.

*I could hear Tiffany's call waiting clicking again. I glanced at my
watch—somehow we had talked for two hours. "See, I told you it was
a long story. Go ahead, I gotta run anyway."*

*"It's a good story. Really inspiring," she said. "But I still don't know
how I'm going to find another job in fashion."*

*"You don't have to know—that's the point," I said. "You just have to
keep trying." But she had already clicked over to answer Sean's call, and
I wasn't sure if she'd heard what I'd said.*

In Her Own Words: Lisa on Dreams
& Perseverance

Dreams help us soar. When you dream, you can go as far as your imagination goes. Think of the Wright brothers, dreaming to fly. Dreams are how things are created, inventions come about, and companies change the world. Dreams are why people become movie stars or surgeons. They are vital.

But you have to put the work in to make your dreams real. You have to focus, and not get distracted. A dream is only that—it's just a dream. If you don't work on it, it's only potential—and you can have all the potential in the world, but if you don't focus and work hard and persevere, it'll only *ever* be potential. My dream was to have Terrence go to college, and so I focused; I put in the time and support and money that was needed to help him get there. I persevered for twenty years, and he made it.

If you're going to dream, you have to also come up with a plan and work hard. Terrence has become successful, fulfilled his potential and lives his dreams, because he works it like an animal. He sees how his dad and I work like animals. I get up at five in the morning to work at my job. Every day I ask myself,

What is it that I'm doing to propel my company forward today? Did I contact a new customer? Did I try something new? Did I put in the work?

A dream only goes as far as the work, the focus, and the plan behind it. Otherwise it's just a dream.

Kevin Hart Talks About His Mom

Kevin Hart is one of the funniest people I know. He is also one of the smartest businessmen, too. One of the most celebrated names in comedy today, his most recent special Let Me Explain *and tour changed the business model for comedians forever. The resident scene stealer on* Think Like a Man *and* Think Like a Man Too, *Kevin also has a string of films on the horizon, including* Ride Along *with Ice Cube and* About Last Night. *The sky is the limit for Kevin and I'm privileged to call him a friend. Kevin told me about his mom and how tough she was on him. Kevin's mom passed away in 2006, and his love and respect for her are still clear today.*

My mom was overreligious to the point where it was scary. She put God first before anything, and everything had a spiritual side. She was strict, the kind of woman who would beat your ass and then tell you that God told her to do it. It was confusing. But you know what? They don't make them like her anymore. She was strong-minded, independent, and stubborn.

I remember in high school I wanted to play basketball, but to get to practice at 5:30 in the morning I had to catch the bus. It was just too early. My mom told me it wasn't safe. Instead, I set all the clocks in the house forward two hours, so when I left the house at 4 A.M. it

171

looked like I was leaving at 6 A.M. She got to work two hours early. When she realized what I had done, the level of trouble I was in was insane. She whupped my ass, but it was worth it because I made the team.

But because of how strict she was, and the way she stuck to her beliefs, she raised me as a nice, amazing young man. There was no bending with my mom—you'd get home from school and do your schoolwork and go outside for an hour, and then when you were done, you'd come inside and read a book. It was all about learning and education. That's all she believed in. Fun wasn't a priority.

She made sure I was active but in productive activities: I was on the swim team from ages eight to seventeen, three different ball teams, and the track and field team. She wanted to keep me focused. I take that with me to this day, and am the same way with my kids, putting them in everything so they have lots of outlets.

I'm a success today because of her. It all goes back to the work ethic I learned from her. I want to put my all into the things I feel like I can achieve. There's no better reward for hard work than a payoff. I saw it work for her, and now I see it for myself. My goals are high and I feel like if I continue to put my mind to them, I can achieve all of them.

My mom died seven years ago. She was very proud of what I'd achieved. She'd be even prouder now. But she never took credit for my success. After all, she was religious, so she didn't like the cussing.

8

My Mother's Words of Wisdom About Putting Others First

*T*iffany and Sean are over, for real this time. Tiffany called me last night, in tears. "He's been cheating on me for months," she said. "I only found out because the other girl posted about it on her Facebook page, calling me out in front of everyone. I feel like an idiot. He totally played me."

I can't say I was surprised to hear it. And honestly, I had to hope that this was an opportunity for her to get some better influences in her life. Sean had been holding her back from the things she wanted, anyway. But I wasn't going to say that. And it didn't mean it didn't hurt—especially coming only two weeks after she lost her job.

"My life is over," she moaned. "It's like—that whole vision I had, of the three of us raising a family together and me studying fashion and Sean stepping up and being the dad? Wow. I was so stupid."

"You weren't stupid, just optimistic. At least you had a vision."

"*Same thing.*" *Her voice on the other end of the line was high-pitched and screechy.*

I suddenly had a vision of what it was like to be the parent of a teenage girl: very frustrating. "*Come on, now. Visions aren't stupid. Anyway—you and Sean always seemed to want different things. Maybe it's good that you are going to be able to pursue some new directions on your own.*"

"*Pursue new directions? Why bother pursuing anything? Oh, and listen to this—my grandma wants me and Tyler to move out. Says a one-bedroom is just too small for all three of us. So now I'm jobless, loveless, and about to be homeless. I give up.*"

Who was this girl? "*You can't give up. Remember—your personal legend?*"

"*I've got nothing. Nothing.*"

"*You've got Tyler. And you've got yourself. That's not nothing.*"

"*Easy for you to say.*"

Though I could understand why she felt this way, I knew this whiny attitude wasn't going to get her very far. It was frightening to listen to Tiffany talk like this—all these months, despite her very real moments of setback and frustration, she'd always had an upbeat attitude. Now that was gone, replaced by a sense of defeat. But I had to confess that the tone in her voice sounded familiar to me. It sounded suspiciously like how I had sounded when I had a rough time in my midtwenties. And I realized that what she needed was context.

My mom always taught me that putting others first helps you get yourself where you want to go in life—that sometimes, instead of complaining about how bad you have it, you need to look around and remember how much worse it could be. This advice had helped lift me up at a time when I needed it the most. Maybe it was a lesson that could help Tiffany now, too.

ON TUESDAY, JANUARY 12, 2010, a massive earthquake struck Haiti. In less than a minute, the island as we know it was utterly destroyed. A quarter of a million homes were obliterated. Thirty thousand more buildings collapsed, including the Presidential Palace, the National Assembly, and the local United Nations headquarters. The earthquake left 3 million people suffering, 1.5 million homeless (17 percent of the population!)—and more than 316,000 dead.

On the day of the earthquake, I was sitting in my dressing room on the set of *106 & Park*, at the all-time low of my adult life. It had not been a good winter for me.

On the personal front, I was going through a miserable breakup. There's always one breakup in a man's life that really tears him down. This one was completely my fault due to cheating, and it really had an effect on me. And on the work front, *106 & Park* was going through some turmoil. Rocsi and I had replaced two iconic hosts, AJ and Free, and a lot of people hated us just because we weren't them. Living up to the expectations of a number one show was really hard. Bloggers destroyed us, commenters said they hated us, rumors floated about the fate of the show. Ratings dipped, and there were rumors that the show would be canceled.

In addition to all this, I had created one of my biggest problems myself. My finances were a mess. When I first came to *106 & Park*, I thought I'd made it to the top of the food chain, hanging out with celebrities every day. I was doing well for myself—a nice six-figure salary, enough to pay my bills and college loans—but after taxes took their bite, it went fast. And I was hanging around multimillionaires, some barely even out of their teens.

I got sucked into the typical "keeping up with the Joneses" mentality of the entertainment industry. I'd go to a nightclub on a Tuesday, and blow $1,200 on bottle service, just so I could be one of those guys with the sparklers going off and the girls at their table. I went and bought myself chains, an Escalade, an apartment. I treated friends and strangers to fancy dinners.

I couldn't afford any of it. I had great friends and advisers who warned me that I needed to live within my means—mentors like Mike Kyser (president of Atlantic Records) and Chaka Zulu (head of DTP Records). "Pace yourself," Mike Kyser would tell me. "Don't try to show off." Chaka would say, "Save your money, let your money grow." But I didn't listen: I wanted to be living the life, like the guys I encountered every day.

In my first year, I even went to meet with Diddy, one of the first people to take me under his wing, He told me that "work ethic comes first. I live the way I live because of the work I put into my business."

Still, the message didn't resonate. Not yet. I thought that I got the *things* first, and that those *things* would perpetuate the success, instead of the other way around.

To make matters even worse, I had no clue how to do my own taxes as an independent contractor. I had no financial manager; I didn't understand fundamental economics. And thanks to the market crash and housing downturn, the condo I'd bought was turning out to be a bad investment. I even had to turn my car in. I knew what it was like to not have anything, but it's even more embarrassing when you have something and then you squander it away.

And that's when I got audited. I owed massive back taxes. By the time the IRS collected what I neglected to pay, I was totally broke. I had absolutely nothing to show for all the money I'd earned. And if girls were at the root of my motivation, all the reckless spending never led to anything good. If anything, the best women I'd dated, the most loyal, had dated me because I was being myself, not trying to be someone I wasn't.

As a result, I'd spent most of that winter feeling sorry for myself, wanting to give up on everything. And yet I still wasn't changing my ways; I was still trying to live the life. Everything that I was going through really affected me in a negative way. I was aggressive and angry; I would show up late for work. I was always on edge. At this point I was operating purely off of credit cards, just to keep up the appearance that everything was okay. One night I went to a nightclub and bought a bottle, only to have my card declined. Embarrassed and frustrated, I snapped. As I walked out of the club, I punched the first parked car I saw, hitting it so hard that I shattered a window and messed up my hand. I sat on the ground and looked down at my bleeding fist, and I didn't know the man I was becoming.

This all led to an incredible amount of stress, which only further complicated my problems. One day, while getting prepared to go onset, my barber, Marshall, noticed a small patch of light skin on my cheek. Unique, our makeup artist, looked at it and recommended that I check it out with a dermatologist. I ignored her suggestion and carried on as usual, figuring the light patch would just go away. Instead, it started to grow. Another blotch appeared on my hand. And then another on my neck. And then around my eyes. Frustrated and concerned, I finally went to get it checked out. My dermatologist diagnosed me with vitiligo.

Vitiligo is a condition that causes depigmentation of sections of skin. My doctor told me that the cause is unknown, but research suggests that vitiligo can be triggered by stress or bodily deficiencies. It's particularly noticeable in African American skin, and more noticeable whenever you spend any time in the sun. It's the same condition Michael Jackson was diagnosed with.

More light patches, varying in size and shape, started popping up on my arms, back, and midsection. As the patches appeared, I grew more and more stressed out and depressed. Would they consume me and hinder—or destroy—my career on camera? I literally felt myself falling apart, physically, mentally, and financially.

One morning in early January, my mom called me to check in, and I broke down. She listened in her caring, empathetic way as I laid all my problems out for her.

To this day, I can still remember her words to me at this time: "Whenever you think life is at its worst, you need to take a step back and look at the rest of the world; because someone, somewhere, is going through something a lot worse. If you really stop to take a look at other people's problems, you're going to want your own problems back," she said. "You are so blessed, so talented. There are people all over the world who have so much less than you. Instead of looking at the things you don't have, you need to focus on the things that you do have."

She continued: "What you need to do is take time away from your own life to help other people. The more you give, and the more God sees you giving, the more He will bestow upon you. Take your immediate focus off yourself—when it's not *me me me* anymore, but *others others others*, greater things will happen in your life."

My mom was speaking from experience. She was always thinking about others instead of herself, and had ever since I could remember. It was just in her nature: She would give until she couldn't
give anymore.

*On the other end of the line, Tiffany sniffed. "I don't have anything
to give away," she said. "I have no money. I can't even pay my own
bills."*

*"It isn't necessarily about money," I responded. "There are lots of
ways to help others that aren't about money."*

My mother was always donating to local charities—like the Sal-
vation Army, Goodwill, and the local libraries. She helped out with
church drives and holiday car washes. But even more inspiring was
the way she was constantly helping out the people in our community. If a neighbor's lawn mower was broken—a big deal when you
live on an acre of grass and it's the middle of a hot North Carolina
summer—my mom would simply drive her own mower across the
street and take care of it herself. When a friend landed in financial trouble and was worried about paying for groceries, my mom
helped her find a meal delivery program. If kids were selling Girl
Scout cookies, my mom would buy three boxes. When a friend's
kid headed off to college, she would give them $50 to buy books.
If a lonely old lady stopped her in the grocery store, just wanting
someone to talk to, my mom would sit and chat with her as if she
had all the time in the world to spend talking to a needy stranger.

As my mom puts it, "That's what the world is about—trying to help people out the best you can."

It is the little things that count, sometimes. I remember in high school, a friend of mine desperately wanted her driver's license. But she lived with her grandmother, who didn't have a car; so she had no way of learning. My mom volunteered to teach her how to drive using her own car. She took my friend down to a local mall and spent hours letting her practice her parallel parking and left-hand turns in the parking lot.

Even animals were the recipients of her largesse. Her philosophy was that food should never be wasted; so the leftovers we didn't or couldn't eat were given to the local animals. She left stale bread and leftover stew by the back door so often that our house was a regular parade of cats, squirrels, possums, rabbits, and deer.

"We are stewards. It's our responsibility to take care of anything we have the ability to take care of." I can't remember the number of times she said these words when I was growing up. And I took lessons from her example.

At the radio stations where I'd worked, I had my first exposure to the idea of community giving. Radio stations are constantly doing all kinds of drives: turkey drives, coat drives, raising money for AIDS research. In high school and college, through my work with the radio stations, I was constantly involved with community fund-raising. After I saw what an impact the Unity March that I participated in had on our college community, I began volunteering to go out to talk to high school students about the need to end violence among young people.

And then, when I joined Omega Psi Phi, I was introduced to an amazing organization: the Boys & Girls Club. Our fraternity was heavily involved with the local chapter, and we raised money for PlayStations for their game room. Soon, I found myself mentoring kids and speaking at Boys & Girls Club events. It was the beginning of a relationship that I value to this day.

In New York City, working for BET, I was still volunteering occasionally with the Boys & Girls Club. But by January of 2010, when my mom laid her lecture on me, I was spending a lot more time worrying about my own life than worrying about anyone else's. I'd watched Rocsi do charity work in her hometown of New Orleans, and told myself that I was also doing my part to help others, but honestly, any charity work I was doing now was done out of a sense of obligation or for an event. I hadn't taken it upon myself to get actively engaged in a community on my own.

I heard what my mom said that day, but I didn't really absorb it. Instead, I went on feeling sorry for myself, completely distracted by the issues of my life. Instead of trying to figure out a better way to give back, I spent my time and money on buying expensive sneakers and ordering bottle service at nightclubs.

And then the earthquake happened.

On the day of the Haiti earthquake, the entire staff of BET immediately jumped into action, including us over at *106 & Park*. My job that day was to go on television and spread the word about what was taking place in the Caribbean, off the coast of Cuba. Many of our viewers had relatives in Haiti, and much of what I was doing consisted of delivering messages for people in Haiti who wanted their families in America to know they were safe. The phones may have been down, but certain messages were getting to media outlets; at BET, we spent all day collecting names and news and then going on live TV to share what we'd learned.

"The Joseph family in Port-au-Prince is alive—they have no power and no lights, but they are alive," I would read. "The Duval family wants everyone in New York City to know they are doing okay."

As I delivered these messages, giving our viewers these precious bits of information, I grew more and more engulfed in the story. The news kept pouring in, along with the first images of the devastated country. My contributions to the crisis in Haiti began to feel negligible at best—sure, I was helping disseminate the news, passing on critical messages, but couldn't I be doing more? Millions of people were dead, homeless, helpless. Every message on the television was from organizations like the Red Cross asking people to donate time, donate money, donate resources, donate help.

As I watched the news reports live from Haiti, I felt like the newscasters were talking to me. My mom's words earlier that month began to resonate. "Whenever you think life is at its worst, you need to take a step back and look at the rest of the world; because someone, somewhere, is going through something a lot worse." Well, it couldn't get much worse than what they had going on in Haiti. My own problems were laughable in comparison.

"I remember seeing that, on TV," Tiffany said. She suddenly sounded chastened. "It looked awful."

"In person it was even worse than you could have imagined, but I'll get to that."

This was the opportunity my mom was talking about. It was time to step out of my comfort zone, time to put aside the bullshit that was in my life. It was time—as my mom had put it—to make my life about "others others others." But there was so much to be done in Haiti—what exactly could I offer?

The answer didn't come to me immediately. It took a few months for me to realize what I wanted to do. Finally, I marched into my boss's office and asked for a leave of absence. I was going to go to Haiti.

Over the course of the next three months, Fred and I organized a trip to Haiti with three of our best friends—an old friend named Jamel, a coworker named Deirdre, and my cameraman pal Dave. We bought plane tickets, using our own money. At the time, there were so many organizations with shady reps working out of Haiti that it was difficult to know who to align ourselves with. So we decided to wing it instead—we would have a direct, personal response with whatever Haitians we encountered. We would offer some actual help on the ground, and—using Dave's camera—document our experience in order to inspire people back home to help out, too.

Before leaving, we raised $10,000 in donations to use to help the people we encountered. And then, we jumped on an airplane to Haiti.

The experience I had there would completely change my perspective on my life, and on the world.

Even before the plane landed, I was already feeling inspired. Sitting next to me on the plane was a woman from California named Nicole, who was on her way to teach the people of Haiti how to build their own houses. Her husband was a contractor, and they had collected several hundred thousands of dollars in donated building supplies: wood, hammers, nails, anything you might need to actually build a house. It was the classic concept of "give a man a fish and he'll eat for one night, but teach a man to fish and he'll eat for life." If the people knew how to build their own houses, they wouldn't be so reliant on the authorities to help them. She impressed me, and I was already excited about the way we might be able to help, too. We decided to team up.

Immediately upon landing, we could see that the environment was *way* worse than we could have imagined. Flying in, you could see the devastation stretching out into the horizon, no matter in which direction you looked. The cities were rubble, for miles and miles. The tent camps where the people were living looked like giant trash heaps.

After disembarking from the plane, we drove to a tent city on a plot of land three hours outside of Port-au-Prince, where Nicole planned to build two model homes. But when we arrived at the shipping dock at customs where her building materials were being held, we were confronted by a group of Haitian renegades carrying machine guns. Waving the guns in our faces, they said that if we wanted to collect our supplies, it was going to cost $50,000.

As Nicole wept with frustration, we tried to reason with them. It turns out there's no reasoning with someone with a gun. Their response was "Give us the money or get the fuck out." (We would later learn that many of the supplies that had been sent to help the people of Haiti were being held in customs, essentially for ransom. In a terrible situation, corruption was making everything worse. Nicole would end up going back to the United States to try to get the government involved, but her supplies were never released.)

I remember the feeling of defeat—we had come up with a plan, a real way to help, but even our best intentions couldn't resolve this situation. I'd never felt so powerless in my life.

With our first plan of attack thwarted, we headed to the tent cities, to check out the conditions there and see how we could help.

The tent camps were horrifying. Many of the "tents" were make-shift structures of sticks, tarps, and pieces of plastic held together with string. Families of eight or nine were living in spaces no bigger than my closet at home. They were barely subsisting—living with very little food or without food or clean water, electricity, changes of clothing, or roofs over their heads. Women were afraid to visit the common showers for fear of rape. Without outhouses, people had to relieve themselves on the ground right next to where they slept. The torrential Haitian rain regularly turned the whole place into mud pits, destroying the few possessions that people still owned. Everywhere you looked, people were starving.

And more than a million people were living like this.

We desperately wanted to give these people things, but we hadn't been allowed to bring anything but clothes with us. So we used what money we had to buy any supplies we could get our hands on: rice, bottled water, granola bars. We walked through the tent cities talking to the people we'd meet and handing out trail mix. One woman simply handed me her baby as she started grabbing all the supplies she could, then made me walk her back to her tent. I remember a pregnant woman who ran up to us, looking for food, and the look of anguish on her face when she found out we'd just given out the last of our granola bars. It was devastating.

There was construction going on everywhere as the country tried to rebuild, but the problems were overwhelming. They needed schools, roads, hospitals. The entire infrastructure of the country had been compromised. We began to realize that, as regular folks, our biggest objective was staying out of the way. What the country needed most was professionals: doctors, educators, construction workers.

It was frustrating: I wanted to help, but it was so complicated, so political, even dangerous. I wasn't a doctor or a contractor, I was just an entertainer, but I did my best, gave my time, and put my money where my mouth was. I realized that what I could *really* do was go back to the States and use my profile to raise awareness and generate funds that could go to worthwhile projects.

I met a lot of incredible people during that first trip to Haiti, but the person who affected me the most was a fifteen-year-old earthquake survivor named Sophia. We were walking down a street in Port-au-Prince when I suddenly heard a sweet girl's voice singing Justin Bieber's "Baby." It stopped me in my tracks. How on earth, in the middle of all this destruction and despair, could someone be singing?

The voice belonged to Sophia, who just a few months earlier had lost both her parents in the earthquake. She had been trapped under the rubble for three days, before she had finally been rescued. Now, this little girl was single-handedly taking care of her four-year-old brother, taking any odd job that might help her provide them both with food and shelter. It was an incredibly grown-up responsibility for such a young girl.

When we asked her what she wanted from life, she told us that what she really longed to do was go to school. "I want to be able to read books," she told us. I remember how spoiled I suddenly felt. I thought of the shelves of books I had at home, books that I barely even looked at, and realized how much I took them for granted. How much I took *everything* for granted.

Then we asked her, what have you learned from being in this situation? She said, "I still believe in God, it's all a part of His plan."

Tiffany was quiet on the other end of the line. "She seriously said that? After her parents had died? Wow."

I know—I couldn't believe it. Her circumstances couldn't have been worse, and yet she had an incredibly positive outlook on life. Witnessing her faith and optimism made me realize that I really needed to change my own tune.

I saw, with clear eyes, what my mom had been telling me: how blessed my life really was, how small my problems truly were. The people of Haiti were incredibly resilient. Despite living through conditions that would have most Americans believing it was the end of the world, these people weren't giving up. Instead, they were singing and praying and figuring out how to make the best out of the hand they were dealt. They still had hope. They still had faith.

I had a lot to learn from them. That was when I realized that this wasn't just about me giving to them. They were giving right back to me.

A few days later, we were on our way back home to the United States. Our flight had an overnight layover in Miami. We hadn't taken a shower during our entire time in Haiti—relying instead on sponge baths and a lot of deodorant—and it seemed like a good idea to take a day to clean up and get "unwired" from our trip. So we checked in to a stylish hotel called the Mondrian.

It turned out to be a terrible mistake. Less than twenty-four hours earlier, we had been looking at people sleeping on pieces of cardboard, a few feet away from buckets of their own urine. Now, we were watching Americans in designer clothes eating steaks and spending obscene amounts of money on cocktails. It's crazy to realize how much food people waste. I was totally repulsed.

Watching them, I suddenly understood—*I* was one of the people that I was seeing around me. *I* was the guy who bought bottles at the club, wore piles of jewelry, drove an obnoxious car. *I* had a gold chain around my neck, wore a fancy watch. *I* didn't think twice about spending hundreds of dollars on clothes I'd only wear a few times.

"I can't believe this is my life," I thought as I looked around me. "I can't believe I've been spending this kind of money on this stuff."

My mind had opened. And from that moment on, my life began to change.

In the upcoming months, I began to really rethink my priorities. For the first time, I had a real sense of what's important and what's not. Now, instead of letting those superficial, material things consume me, I stopped being so frivolous, stopped buying fancy jewelry, and stopped whining about problems that, in the grand scheme of things, could be worked out.

I started getting treatment for my vitiligo. The visible conditions fluctuate due to the sun, but in my case, my skin was also affected by stress, diet, and my lifestyle. It is a condition that I may live with for the rest of my life, but it is manageable with special treatments. I can conceal the major outbreaks with makeup while I'm on TV, but I've also come to accept myself and my skin, and learned to embrace what God has given me. Having vitiligo has taught me a valuable lesson about vanity and helped me move beyond it. It has truly allowed me to see the beauty in all people—regardless of their shape, size, or color.

I started getting other aspects of my life in order: I refinanced my mortgage, got a financial manager, and—most important—took a genuine interest in understanding finance. I may have blown everything during the first few years of my career, but because of the mistakes I'd made, I now had a vast understanding of how everything worked. I needed that lump to the head to realize what I'd really been doing.

Don't get me wrong: I still like the finer things in life. I'd be hypocritical if I pretended to turn my nose up at nice cars, jewelry, or having a good night out. But now, when I do, it's for different motives: out of an appreciation for life, not because I need to impress other people or feel validated in some way.

I had a new perspective, and a new lease on life. I was finally turning from a boy into a man.

And it turned out to be just the beginning of a new relationship with the world around me. Not long after I returned, we posted our video "The Haiti Project" on YouTube, and did everything we could to get national coverage for our endeavor. To raise awareness, we spoke to TV news outlets, magazines, blogs, and online forums—anywhere I could encourage people to get involved with helping Haiti. We also started raising funds for Project Medishare, a nonprofit that was providing health services to Haitians and operating a clinic to treat the cholera epidemic.

It was the first time that I had used my celebrity to give back; and now that I'd had an epiphany about the good that I could do, I couldn't wait to do more.

As I wrote to my fans in an online diary on my website:

I challenge you to try to make a difference in your own communities. With a roof, food, clean water, and clothes on our backs, we are more fortunate than millions. If you are reading this online, you are one of the privileged. Please ask yourself, What am I giving back to the world for my blessings? You don't have to be Obama, Oprah, or Angelina Jolie to make a positive impact on others. If it's making an extra sandwich and giving it to the homeless person you always see on the subway, or volunteering with children whose parents can't afford tutoring, you and your friends can create your own personal missions if you just try.

And take my word for it, whatever you give, whatever you donate, your interaction with people less fortunate than you will make your life that much richer. I went on this trip to help the people of Haiti, but it was the people of Haiti who helped me.

And I truly did begin to live by that credo. After that trip, volunteer missions became part of my DNA. Not only did I return to Haiti three times, but I also began to work with other nonprofit organizations. I became the face of the McDonald's African American Scholarship program—giving out a half-million dollars of scholarships every year. I worked with Steve Harvey's Disney Dream Academy, visiting high schools and giving presentations to kids about going to college and chasing their dreams. I set up education workshops and helped high school seniors fill out college applications. I became a director of responsibility for Crown Royal, talking to young people about alcohol abuse at shelters and AA meetings. We implemented the Crown Life Safe Rides Initiative, a program built to make sure people got home safe from the clubs.

(I'd learned from my mistakes.) And I donated thousands of dollars in clothing and sneakers—everything I wore on TV—to benefit foster homes and kids in need.

And of course, there's still the Boys & Girls Club.

I often think of my mom's words: "The more you give, and the more God sees you giving, the more He will bestow upon you." My life has never been richer, and I know that's because of what she inspired me to give away. I'm not doing this to make myself look good. Helping others makes me feel good.

In Her Own Words: Lisa on the Importance of Giving to Others

I have a favorite picture of Terrence, from when he went to Haiti. He's holding a tiny baby in his arms, looking out at the horizon with such concern. It's such a great juxtaposition of the strong male and the innocent helpless baby.

Putting others first builds a strong foundation, strong communities. It's important for young men to think about the world as a whole, and not just focus on themselves. When you see men acting responsible and as positive role models working to help better their communities and the world, then the world feels like a better place. There is less crime, less fear, less violence.

It's like if you're in a burning building and you see a big strapping man coming to get you out, you feel good! Save us!

Giving to others helps you channel your positive energy. Someone is always in a worse situation than you are. Sometimes what you're complaining about is not that important. There are people who need your help more than you need anyone else's. Sometimes giving to others just a little bit—it doesn't have to be a lot—can help you take your mind off the petty things that you're consumed with.

Young men need to go to their local soup kitchen, homeless shelter, Boys & Girls Clubs; they need to see what's going on in their community and try to get involved. There's more to the world than what's happening in your little backyard. When you go out in the world and see what others are facing—not having clean water to drink, when you're out drinking fancy bottled water, for example—you realize that what you might be complaining about doesn't really matter.

It's a kind of grace.

Gary Owen Talks About His Mom

Gary Owen is a comedian and actor who got his big break at BET just like I did. He's headlined comedy tours, starred on Tyler Perry's hit TV show House of Payne, *and costarred with me in* Think Like a Man. *Gary's talent is a force to be reckoned with. He was kind enough to share some stories about his mom, as he treated me to some all-you-can-eat sushi (don't ask).*

My mom is literally the nicest person I've ever met. No one ever says anything bad about her. To this day, all the kids go to her: You're short on rent, she slides you the extra money. She's the epitome of the word "mother": She works, she cooks, she cleans the house. If something happened to her, the rest of my family wouldn't know how to function. She has that kind of hold on everybody.

Anything I did, she was behind me, even if she probably thought it was a pipe dream. When I became a comedian, I was in the military. I made the call and said, "Mom, I'm getting out of the military to be a comic." And she was all, "Oh, that's great! That's good." Any other mom would have been, "What???"

She's like that with all her kids—she never has anything negative to say. Even if one of her kids isn't doing as well as another, she makes us all feel like we're progressing in life. One kid's on drugs, and is going to rehab: "You're doing good, taking steps! You're going to rehab!" She makes you feel good about *that*!

She puts everyone before herself, almost to a fault. My mom had me when she was in high school. It was just me and her. We had a bond that was special. But we didn't have a lot, growing up. I remember living in an apartment with one living room and one bedroom, and at age four she asked me if I wanted the bedroom or the living room. I chose the living room, because of the TV—but if I'd wanted the bedroom, she would have taken the couch. That's her most endearing quality—she's more concerned about what you want.

One day, when I was seven or so, we were driving on the highway, and the car broke down. We were hot, somewhere in the middle of nowhere in Ohio. I remember popping the hood, and the engine was smoking everywhere. I looked at it and told her, "Mom, when I grow up I'm going to buy you an engine." Not a car! An engine! I always remembered her laughter.

So last year, I bought her a new car for Mother's Day. I said, "Mom, remember when I said I was going to buy you a new engine?" And I walked her into the front yard, where there was a new car waiting for her. It was a great moment.

9

My Mother's Words of Wisdom
About Patience & Humility

*C*hristmas in New York is unparalleled, and I was glad to be
back. I'd flown into town for a few days for work, and while
I was there, I decided to drop in on the Boys & Girls Club. I
missed everyone, and I particularly wanted to check in on Tiffany, who
I hadn't spoken with since our last conversation, six weeks earlier.

She wasn't there, so I sent her a text—Hey, I'm at the B&G Club,
come by if you're around.

Forty-five minutes later, while I was in the middle of a pickup basketball game with some of the boys, I noticed Tiffany sitting over on the
sidelines, with Tyler in her lap playing with a toy car, her sketchbook
open next to her as she tried to draw with her free hand. I was glad to
see that notebook again.

When the game was over, I wandered over and sat next to her. She
looked great—she'd dressed up in jeans and a cute striped top that

looked like she'd made it herself, and little Tyler was in a perfectly matching outfit, also homemade. He was squirming all over her lap, dying to get onto the court and crawl after the basketball.

"Before you start getting that worried look on your face, I'm okay," she said. *"I'm moving back down to Atlanta. My mom's sister offered to let me move in with her. She has a spare bedroom in her apartment now that my cousin got married and moved out."*

"That's great," I said tentatively.

She put Tyler down on the floor and watched him immediately crawl away, looking for trouble. "He's such a boy. It's all about balls and music already." *She smiled and looked back at me.* "Anyway, yeah. Atlanta makes a lot of sense. It's cheaper there. And my cousin offered to watch Tyler with her own kids."

"What about work?"

"I'm going to work at my uncle's restaurant." She looked abashed. *"I know. It's not fashion. But I did find a school that has night classes in fashion design, so I'm going to try to do that, too."*

She jumped up and ran after Tyler, who was in danger of being trampled by the ballplayers. When she came back, with him wriggling under her arm, she sat down next to me and continued, "Remember how we talked about *The Alchemist, and the whole personal legend thing? Well, I decided that I needed to keep dreaming. And I was just spinning my wheels here in New York. So I thought maybe I'd mix things up."*

I smiled. "I think it's the right move. Small steps."

"More like baby steps." She grimaced. "At this rate I'll be a hundred before I ever get there."

But life doesn't always happen all at once. I knew a little bit about how being patient and humble can help you get where you want to go. If you aren't ashamed to start small, you can end up somewhere very big.

GROWING UP IN NEW York City, we couldn't afford a car. When we went anywhere, it was on the bus. The bus system, however, wasn't particularly reliable. Sometimes my mom and I would sit at the bus stop for what felt like hours, waiting for a bus to come along.

It drove me absolutely nuts. I would be tearing my hair out, dying to run around, whining at the top of my lungs. But my mom would just sit there quietly, with her hands in her lap, never complaining.

"Have patience," she'd remind me. "Patience is key. People who don't have patience never amount to anything."

I didn't like to hear it at the time, but something must have sunk in. Because, looking back, it's clear that one of the biggest successes I've had in my life is due to the patience that I learned from her.

By 2009, I'd been working at *106 & Park* for three years. I loved my job but secretly still longed to do some acting. I'd started taking acting workshops at the Lee Strasberg Institute, and had taken some small parts in independent movie projects that friends had produced, but I had yet to win a role in any kind of Hollywood production.

I'd recently become involved in the Disney Dreamers Academy. Once a year, the Disney Dreamers Academy gathers a hundred disadvantaged kids from around the country and flies them to Orlando, Florida, for a weekend of mentoring and Disney fun. It's a great organization. That year, the academy's selection process was taking place at the home of Steve Harvey, one of the academy's founders, and I was invited to participate.

I knew who Steve Harvey was from *The Kings of Comedy*—and I was a huge fan. And he also happened to be a fraternity brother, a fellow member of Omega Psi Phi. I was thrilled at the chance to meet him, and when I arrived at his enormous house I was welcomed with open arms.

Steve and I spent a lot of time bonding that weekend, but one particular thing that he said really stuck with me, because it reminded me of something my mom had always told me, too: "In life, it's all about relationships." "Never burn bridges," he said. "Always keep your relationships close, and take care of them." This is advice that would serve me well in the coming years.

The Dreamers Academy was an incredible experience—and I've stayed involved ever since. The kids were really inspiring to work with. While doing a mentor session, I ended up sitting on a panel next to a young Hollywood producer named Will Packer, an inspiring person who would also end up being very influential in my life.

Fast forward to August of 2009. It was the five-year anniversary of my fraternity line brothers' graduation, and all thirteen of us had decided to fly to Las Vegas to celebrate. Steve Harvey had invited me to present at the Hoodie Awards, an annual award event he hosts. Think of the Hoodie Awards as a kind of Oscars: Essentially, he honors the best neighborhood barber shops, the best soul food, the best hair and nail salons, the best teachers, the best church choirs. It's all about average, everyday heroes, with the celebrities presenting the awards to everyday men instead of receiving the awards themselves. It's an enormously popular event.

The night of the awards, I was in a great mood. My fraternity brothers were in the crowd, and as I walked onstage to present an award, the song that began to blare over the loudspeakers was "Atomic Dog" by George Clinton—a song that just happens to be Omega Psi Phi's fraternity song, complete with a special hop (a choreographed dance). So when I heard the first bars coming over the sound system, I ripped my shirt off, ran into the crowd, and found my fraternity brothers. Together, we spontaneously began to dance. The crowd went nuts.

My antics paid off, because Will Packer was in the crowd that day with a gentleman named Clint Culpepper, the president of Sony Screen Gems. Together, they had just acquired the film rights to Steve Harvey's book *Act Like a Lady, Think Like a Man*. They were at the Hoodie Awards to announce the upcoming movie adaptation, and they witnessed me working the crowd into a frenzy.

After the event we attended the after party, which was an all-white party. I was standing backstage, wearing a white seersucker suit with a fresh pair of white bucks straight from the box. You couldn't tell me nothing that day. As I stood there with the fellas, Will Packer came over with Clint Culpepper in tow. Clint immediately admired my shoes and shook my hand. "Where in the hell did you get that suit?" he asked.

I whispered to him, "Barneys. But the tag is still in it, in case I have to bring it back." He let out a laugh.

"You have so much charisma," he said. "I want to put you in a movie."

Tiffany looked impressed. "Seriously? You were discovered by a Hollywood producer? That's like, living the dream."

I laughed. "That's not exactly how it happened."

"I want to put you in a movie" may be the most hollow words in Hollywood. People say this all the time, and rarely—if ever—do they actually follow up. But I remembered the advice I'd gotten from my mom and Steve Harvey—"nurture your relationships." So I kept in touch. I sent Clint and Will holiday greetings at Christmas; cordial emails just to say hello. I kept my name in their consciousness. Over time, as you continue to communicate with people, you start to develop genuine relationships with them; and after a while, my friendship with them became organic. I wasn't hitting on them because I wanted a gig, but because over time you truly become friends.

Those relationships started to manifest into amazing things. Within six months, I got a call from Shayla Cowan, Will Packer's right hand. Will was putting together a sequel to his hit movie *Stomp the Yard*, about step competitions at a black university. Shayla set up an audition for me with the casting director. I jumped at the opportunity, worked on the audition with my acting coach, and flew out to audition for the second lead.

I didn't get the part. Instead, they offered me a much smaller part, four or five characters down the list. My manager at the time told me that I should turn it down. "It's a direct-to-video movie," he sniffed. "You're on TV every day. You're a name. You need to either be a lead or a more prominent role. There's no reason to take the role they're offering."

This is the kind of ego-stroking thing that managers say all the time. And I *did* want a bigger role. I would need to take almost three weeks off work to do the movie, which was a lot of time for a role that wouldn't even get me prominent placement.

But I stopped and remembered my mom. My mom was always humble. My parents didn't expect anything fancy. They were minimalists. It was about what was necessary, not what was lavish. Humility, not cockiness, was what they valued.

"I want to do it," I told my manager. "I really want to work with Will Packer. I'll take any role they offer me. I don't care what it is."

My boss at BET, Stephen Hill, was terrific about letting me take time off to do *Stomp the Yard 2*. But there was a lot of travel involved. I would literally be in dance rehearsals in Atlanta all day, learning the moves and filming scenes, then get on a nine o'clock flight back to New York City, film my *106 & Park* segments, and then fly back to Atlanta on the red-eye. Three or four times a week! By the time I was done with filming, I'd spent more than double on airplane tickets than I'd actually been paid for acting in the movie.

But it was well worth the time and effort, because I got to spend more time getting to know Will Packer; Shayla; and the film's director, Rob Hardy. We even spent Thanksgiving together in Atlanta—I was too tapped out to fly back to New York City for the holiday. Even though the movie didn't change my life financially, it ended up being a great experience. I developed new relationships, got experience on camera, and learned all about being on a movie set.

In early December, just a few weeks after we wrapped *Stomp the Yard 2*, I got a call from Clint Culpepper. He had a role for me in a film, playing Cher's assistant in *Burlesque*. He was a man of his word: He was putting me in my first Hollywood movie. It was the most exciting thing in the world.

I went back to Stephen Hill and asked him for a few more days off, to fly out to L.A. and shoot the part. This time, he said no. "You already used all your time," he said.

I was floored. "I just need a few days."

"I just gave you three weeks."

It grew more heated. Next thing I knew, we were yelling at each other. I could hear myself, sounding like a teenager complaining that his dad is being unfair. "You need to make a decision," he said. "You are the anchor of this show. We need you here. You have a great job and you need to appreciate that more."

He told me to get out of his office. I slammed the door, cursed at him on the way out, and told him I was leaving. I'm not sure what I meant by that, and I don't think he knew, either.

I walked back to my dressing room and looked around. Was this it? I grabbed my things and made a halfhearted attempt at packing up, and then slumped to the ground. I didn't know what to do. Legally and morally, he was right. I had no argument. I'd taken off all the days at work I possibly could. But I really wanted to work on this project, to begin my career as an actor and begin building my brand outside BET. After working so hard to nurture that relationship, I was embarrassed to go back and tell Clint I couldn't take the roll. But I also loved my job at *106 & Park*. And the more I thought about it, the more I felt horrible about the way I'd yelled at Stephen. He was well within his rights to tell me no.

This time, I didn't even have to call my mom to know what she was going to say to me. She would have told me the same thing that she told me at NASCAR: "If you believe in something and your heart is saying you have to do it, then you have to do it. No matter what the sacrifice is." She would have told me that I needed to humble myself a little and go apologize to Stephen Hill. "You have to be a man if you want to be treated like a man," I could hear her say. "Go back and work it out."

She would have been right, of course. So I called Antoinetta, Stephen Hill's assistant at the time, and asked her to set up a meeting. She told me that he was really upset and needed some time. I gave him a few hours before going back to his office.

The first thing I did was tell him how sorry I was for being disrespectful. "You changed my life," I said. "I don't know where I'd be without you and *106*. But I need to do this, its part of my long-term life plan. What can I leverage to make this happen?"

He took me in for a minute, and then finally laughed. "Look, if you ever curse at me and slam my door again, you'll be out on the street faster than you got here." He paused. "So I guess if you're going to do this no matter what, we'll figure it out."

And we did figure it out—a few weeks later, I flew out to L.A. and shot three days with Cher and Christina Aguilera. He did make me pay for those three days: I was indebted to him for the rest of my time at *106 & Park*. But I learned a lot from that encounter.

From that point on, we were friends instead of just employee and employer; I wasn't just the talent, I was participating in the show as a producer, too. I had gained his respect as a businessman by humbling myself and trying to work things out. I wasn't afraid of my boss anymore. Instead, I realized that a good working relationship is about figuring things out together, compromising, being in a partnership. To this day, I can call on Stephen as a mentor and friend, and we still do a lot of business together.

And the film that I was willing to sacrifice my job for? It was an amazing experience—my first time on the set of a major Hollywood film—and worth every bit of grief I got.

Tyler had squirmed off Tiffany's lap again and was attempting to overturn a garbage can. Tiffany ran to retrieve him and then came back and sat next to me again. "I didn't know you were in Burlesque," *Tiffany said. "I loved that movie."*

"I played Dave the DJ."

Neither of these roles—a small role in a small film, and an even smaller role in a big film—was going to knock the world's socks off. But it's all about the slow build, about *patience.* This whole time, during the filming of those movies and the events surrounding their release, I was building relationships. *Nurture your relationships.*

Three years after we met at the Hoodie Awards, Clint and Will were ready to put *Think Like a Man* into production. Shayla was on the ground with that production, and she kept me abreast of what was going on; it's thanks to her that I was slipped one of the earliest copies of the script, before anyone else had it.

As soon as I got the script, I knew I wanted to do this film. I bought a copy of Steve's book. Wherever I was—in my bedroom, my dressing room—I would read it. Every time I looked at the cover I'd say to myself, "I am going to be in this movie." I read the script over and over and over again.

One Monday morning, not long afterward, Will called me. "Hey, man," he said. "I know this is last minute, but we're having a table read for *Think Like a Man* tomorrow. Are you in L.A. right now? Because we'd love to have an extra voice."

"Of course I'm in L.A.," I told him. "I'll see you tomorrow morning, bright and early. Looking forward to it, man."

I got off the phone with him, confused. I had no idea what a table read was. Not to mention the fact that I was still in New York. I hit Fred immediately and told him to go on Kayak.com and buy us two coach tickets on the next thing smoking. I faked sick—by now, my signature move—on the phone to my executive producer. On the way to Los Angeles, in middle seat 38B, I read and reread the part I'd been assigned: Michael, a momma's boy. By the time we landed, I had it memorized, as if I was going to be tested on it the next day. After all, the same stuff you do in school is the same stuff you do out of school.

When I walked into the table read, I was thrilled to discover that the director was Tim Story. I had auditioned for him for a pilot two years earlier. Even though I hadn't gotten that part, he remembered me, and we had an instant rapport. It goes to show that things often come full circle.

A table read, I soon discovered, was not an audition at all. It was simply a read-through of the script, so that the production team can hear how the jokes sound and the script reads. The whole team was there, watching. When I was handed my script, I just stuck it under the table. I didn't need it: I knew the script by heart. Some of the other actors read their parts straight; others put a little bit of pepper on it. Me? I was acting out every scene as if a camera was coming in for my close-up. I didn't know any better. I put everything I had into it. Maybe it wasn't a formal audition, but this was *my* audition. I knew they were going to go look for a bigger actor, so this was the only chance I was going to get.

After the reading, Will pulled me aside. Will is extremely charismatic and he has a way of making any news, even when it's not the greatest, sound like you just won the lotto. "Thanks so much for coming. You did a great job. We need big names for the lead roles, but we're definitely going to find something for you," he said, with all the charm in the world.

"Thanks, Will!" I said. It took me three days to realize what he really meant—I probably wasn't getting this role. Damn.

Fast forward to six months later, and I'm on the set of *Think Like a Man*, getting to work under the direction of Tim Story alongside super movie and TV stars that I'd looked up to for years. My role? Michael, the same part that I'd read months earlier—the same part they said they were going to give to a bigger actor. The movie outdid anyone's expectations; it ultimately went on to make just under $100 million—almost ten times its budget. In addition to the film's success, *Think Like a Man* went on to win the BET Award for Best Movie. Walking onstage to accept the award from BET, the company that had started my career all those years earlier, was one of the most gratifying moments I could ever have imagined. The only thing that made it even better? I would soon get the chance to reprise my role in a sequel.

But up until the minute the camera rolled, I was still convinced that someone was going to walk into my trailer and say, "It's all a practical joke. Did you really think you got this role?"

There are a lot of reasons why Clint and Will changed their minds and gave me the part, even though they had other actors in mind. At the top of the list was the fact that I came into the table read and just owned that character. I had studied and studied, worked and worked at it—just like my mom taught me—until I had willed it into my existence. As my mom says, *the more you work, the luckier you'll get.*

But there were other reasons, too.

I got the job because of relationships. I'd nurtured my connection with Will and Clint, growing a business relationship that over time led to a genuine and close friendship. When it came down to it, they were willing to take a risk on me.

I think another reason I may have gotten the gig was because of my humility. My manager thought I was too big to take that first job on *Stomp the Yard 2*, but I never came in cocky. I was grateful for any opportunity I received, and I came in humble, as if I was an intern starting at the bottom. And you know what? That small role in that small movie ultimately started my acting career in earnest.

And last, I got the job because of patience. *Think Like a Man* was almost four years in the making, and I had the patience to wait for it to manifest. In this industry, things don't happen overnight. I went to over a hundred auditions for roles I didn't get. Success doesn't often come from your first audition or casting call, and your ego is going to get bruised and damaged along the way. But all you can do is plant those seeds and wait for them to grow.

Like my mom also said, *patience is key*. No matter how long she had to wait, that bus always eventually arrived and got her where she wanted to go. And it did the same for me.

I glanced at my watch—it was time for me to leave. Before I left, I stood up and gave Tiffany a hug—I had no idea when I would see her next. Tyler batted at my face with his little baby hands. "Good luck, little man," I told him. "I'll be expecting to hear big things coming from you soon."

In Her Own Words: Lisa on Patience & Humility

We're in a world now where it is all about instant gratification. But sometimes it takes a long time to master something. Things don't come to you overnight. You have to put in the time. You really have to have patience. Today, a lot of kids struggle with that.

I didn't learn all the things I'm telling you overnight. This has taken years, and I'm still working at the Art of Learning. I'm still always trying to perfect things. Sometimes we want things so quickly—or we think we do—and we have to calm down and put the time in. In creating a company, for example—you're not going to be able to get your website up in a day, order your business cards, launch your advertising. Rome wasn't built in one day. Instead, you need to come up with a plan for what you want to do, and then take it one day at a time. That takes patience.

Many kids today feel very entitled. They think they deserve to have everything, right away. That's why humility is a value we all need to teach, and learn.

Humility comes from being grateful: Grateful for the sacrifices that other people make for us every day. We only succeed because of the help and assistance we were given along the way. No one makes it totally on their own. When you're given opportunities, you better be thankful, because they could have been given to someone else.

You need to say thank you—to show your gratitude, to let people know *I realize what you did for me and I'm humbled by it. I'm humbled, because you didn't have to do it.*

And I believe this all starts with the mom. I could have been the type of mom who had to get my nails and hair done every week, go to the club every weekend. But I never did those things. I think Terrence realizes *my mom did all these things for me, and I'm humbled and thankful. She sacrificed a lot for me.* And when I go to see my own mom, and remember all the things she sacrificed for me, that humbles me, too.

Moms, your kids need to see this. They need to see more examples of people acting with good behavior. A lot of kids today are followers—they do what they see other people doing. When we are doing good deeds, they will emulate that. They need to see us being humble and grateful and appreciative of what we've been given.

Trey Songz Talks About His Mom

Trey Songz is a Grammy-nominated artist, producer, and actor. Unlike me, Trey was actually discovered by a record producer at a talent show while he was still in high school. (See, it's possible!) He's made five hit albums, starred in Texas Chainsaw 3D, *and appeared with me in* Baggage Claim. *He took the time to share a few memories of his mom with me.*

My mom was strong and stern, yet kind and funny. She always taught me things and corrected me when I was wrong—anything from misbehavior to grammatical errors. She had me at seventeen, so all my life she's been like a big sister as well. We always say we grew up together.

She helped me become the person I am today by setting a great example. There were no men around in my adolescence, and the two that I would typically look to for an example of how to be a man—my father and stepfather—fell short time and time again. My mother would work job after job, and practically sacrificed much of her young life to be a good mother. I'm the man I am because she's the woman she is.

She was willing to make hard decisions for my benefit, ones that really shaped me as a person. After years of travel, she let me move back to Virginia for high school, and it provided the life experience, exposures, and environment I needed to later become Trey Songz. It also gave me my closest friends.

The most inspiring thing she ever said to me was in the early days of my music career. I'd been scammed and turned down before actually being offered a real contract. She told me not to give up, that my time was coming, and to keep honing my craft singing anywhere they would let me.

She was always there for me. I remember a day, when I was young, when we were at the water park and I had somehow slipped through the inner tube. My mom hopped in, clothes on and all, and swooped me up out of that water so fast. I'll never forget that, ever. I have many memories like these, when my mom would show that she would undoubtedly do anything for me.

Epilogue

When my phone rang late last night, my first reaction was to let it go to voice mail—until I saw it was Tiffany on my caller ID. We hadn't talked much in the past few months, both balancing and juggling our busy lives. I was pleasantly surprised to hear from her—even if it was the middle of the night. It's amazing how much has changed since she first called me almost two years ago, freaking out.

She was freaking out as I answered her call—but this time for a much different reason. "Guess what!?" she said, as if she had just heard some juicy gossip.

"I have no idea. Just please don't tell me you're pregnant again," I groggily scoffed back—joking, but not really.

"No, loser," she replied, and proceeded to update me on all of her news.

"Tyler is doing fine. Healthy and happy. He is the true joy of my life and the greatest thing that has ever happened to me," she gushed.

Her aunts and cousins in Atlanta, the family of the mom Tiffany never really knew, have stepped up to give her a hand with Tyler. It takes a village to raise a child, and the trusted support of family has helped her out in ways she couldn't have imagined. I have no doubt that with a mom like Tiffany, Tyler will grow up to be a king. Although things didn't work out with Sean, he does send money to help her, visits when he can, and he and Tiffany have a working friendship.

Tiffany was accepted and is currently enrolled in night classes at the Savannah College of Art and Design, a prestigious college that's the perfect hub to nurture her talents. She's taking a manageable number of classes and enjoying them, and she's surrounding herself with positive, like-minded students.

She also landed a part-time job at the Louis Vuitton store in the mall. Her store manager had taken a liking to Tiffany's unfiltered honesty and keen eye for fashion. Although she works limited hours, her manager gives her tons of "creative control." He recently asked her to design the fall looks window display, and in the pictures she sent, I could see the similarities to her sketches from way back when. Her sassy yet charming New York attitude, her unique perspective, and her complete knowledge of everything fashion quickly earned her a reputation as the "go-to" salesperson in the store.

Unbeknownst to Tiffany, one of her repeat customers happened to be one of Atlanta's top stylists, who had worked on a range of high-profile accounts—from Tyler Perry Productions and Screen Gems to TNT and CNN. (Today, Atlanta is a growing hub for entertainment productions and a prime destination for many top film and TV projects.) Tiffany had developed a relationship with this stylist, providing her with insightful feedback whenever she came in, emailing her when something of interest arrived, and holding a pair of limited shoes to the side from time to time.

This stylist had recently been commissioned to be the head costume designer on a big-budget ensemble production that would be shooting in Atlanta. Tiffany's work ethic, talent, skill at building relationships, and charm were starting to manifest into opportunity. Tiffany Brown, the young single mother from Brooklyn, New York, would be the new costume trainee, working in the wardrobe department for a Hollywood blockbuster. Tiffany's personal legend is just beginning. She thanked me for being there for her and told me I had inspired her. We promised to keep in touch more before hanging up.

As for me, I think it is her—and what she represents—that truly inspires me. And in many ways, my own personal legend is just beginning as well. Professionally, things are going in a great direction. Between movie, television, business, and writing this book, I really feel blessed. But, if anything, it is the time I've spent with Tiffany that has really opened my eyes to the most important things in life.

I recently flew out to North Carolina and surprised my mom for

Mother's Day. It was such fun to see the shock on her face when she opened the door and found me on our doorstep. She still watches me every time she hears I'll be making a TV appearance, but seeing me in person made her really light up.

It was great to see her, because now that I'm living in Los Angeles, I don't get to visit as often as I like. Physically, we're farther apart than we've ever been—a full country between us—and yet I feel like we're closer than we've ever been. Especially writing this book, I've come to understand her in ways I never did before.

I'm not going to pretend that everything has always been perfect between my mom and me. My quick temper, my rush to judgment? That comes from her, too. We're not always "besties."

But I've also realized that the things I fight about with my mom are the same things that make me stronger, help me form my own opinions, and make me the person I am. These moments help me turn the mirror on myself in order to see myself better. An adversary develops greatness—you gotta have someone to play basketball against or you're just gonna be shooting free throws.

And when my mom and I do have disagreements, we are always able to come back together eventually to talk it through, work it out. Of course we do. Because we're a unit, a team—we have been since the day I was born, and will be long after we're both gone.

While I was in Rocky Mount, my mom and I talked about why I was writing this book. Writing it was a hard decision to make: I'm a pretty guarded person, and some of the subjects I've tackled here—my biological father, her teen pregnancy, our interracial household—are ones I've never really talked about before. So I asked her one last time, "Are you sure you want to do this? It's not too late to stop it. I don't want you to be embarrassed by anything I've written."

She looked at me and said, "If any of my stories about the things I went through can inspire or motivate or give courage to a young mother out there, it'll be worth every page written." Typically modest, she was flattered that I thought she was worthy of a book at all. "I feel like you're really honoring me," she confessed.

It's about time. Because the truth is, she's the one who's been honoring me with her presence my entire life.

I love her more than I can possibly express in these pages.

Acknowledgments

Thank you to everyone who helped me out along this journey. There are so many people who have been instrumental in my life and I appreciate you all.

There are a few people I'd like to thank who directly helped me with the making of this book. (Super-sorry if I forgot you here—I was rushing—I'll remember you onstage at the Oscars.) In no particular order, thank you:

To my parents and my family, Spanky (RIP).

To Fred Whitaker, Travis Bond Roseboro, and both their families, and to Gussie and James Harvey and the Harvey family, Aunt Vicki, and Uncle Nate.

To the greatest team in the business: Charles King, Darrell Miller, Amir Shahkhalili, Kirby Kim, Julian Petty, WME, Fox Rothschild, Michael Kyser, Daymond John, Chaka Zulu, Oronde Garrett, Kevin Liles, and the KWL family.

Acknowledgments

To Will Packer, I can't thank you enough. And to Heather Hayslett and the "Packer Posse," Shayla Cowan, Larry Schwartz (you set me up for life!), Keenan Towns, Roderick Blaylock, and all the playmakers at Diageo, the Crown Life, Team Dolla.

To my TLAM family, you are all like brothers, sisters, and/or drunk uncles to me: Clint Culpepper (you are a man of your word!), Tim Story (we got it!), Regina Hall, Kevin Hart, Romany Malco, Michael Ealy, Jerry Ferrara, Gary Owen, Meagan Good, Taraji P. Henson, Gabrielle Union, LaLa Anthony, Jenifer Lewis, Keith Merryman, David A. Newman, and the entire cast and crew, James Lopez, Valerie Sharpe, Scott Strauss, Glenn Gainor, Davia Carter, and the entire Screen Gems team—we did something special!

To the entire fam: Steve Harvey and Rushion McDonald, Shakim Compere (thank you for believing in me), Queen Latifah, David E. Talbert, Zola Mashariki, Cassandra Butcher, Tashana Ventura, Antoinetta Hairston, Dave Joseph, Jocelynn Jacobs, Jamel Davenport, Rocsi, Chantel Christopher, Ryan Shaffer, Yusuf Neville, Alesha Reneé, Monique Hobbs, Lamorne Morris, Lashawn "Quiet" Ray, Kainon Jasper, Amber Rasberry, Jeanette Jenkins, Tracey Moore-Marable, Tony Shellman, Ludacris and the DTP family, Stephen Hill, Debra Lee, Penny Mac, Rick Grimes, Eric Watson, Jason Riley, Big Tigger, Noni Nicolas, Dawn Woodhouse and Derrin Woodhouse, Bryon Cooper, Nick Storm, Scott da Animal and Twizz, Simply Jess, Jared Nixon, Bu Thiam, Sean

"Pecas" Costner, Clue, DJ Prostyle, Angie Martinez, Joey IE, Ellen Brandon-Calhoun, Andrew Fiet, Carmelo Anthony, T.I., Chris Paul and CJ Paul, Salim and Mara Brock Akil, Sean "Diddy" Combs (since day one), James Cruz, Reginald Hudlin, Bryon Phillips, Connie Orlando, Dwight Freeney, Idris Elba, Robi Reed, Tracy "Twinkie" Byrd, Kim Harden, Trey Songz, Javar Gholson, Jamie Foxx (thanks for allowing me at your house parties), Iyonna, Lance Gross and Vincent Martinez, Wayne, Harry, and the entire Hartbeat Productions team, Jump Shot Jay, Jack Nasty, Crystal Johnson, Latisha King, Lauren London, Malcolm Ray, Denaz Green, Juggie, Jeff Sanchez, Bradley Olah, Krystal Brown, Pooch Hall, Kobe, Tyrese, Michael Strahan, Tara August, Mike B, Jacki, and Keesh, Deirdre Maloney, J Rich, my 102 Jamz family, WNAA 90.1, and Soul 92.

To all my Aggies, I love you. To all of my fraternity brothers and Greeks worldwide, especially the Bloody Mu Psi Chapter of Omega Psi Phi, Spring '04. And to the 13 Mirror Images of Survival: Dimitri Yates, Donovan Caves, Richard Patterson, Darnell Reid, Billy McEachern, Jerome Butler, Uche Byrd, Tamario Howze, Charles Biney, Fred Boone, Eric Robinson, Korch Renner, Antreet Connor, and Larry King.

To Janelle Brown (for putting up with me), Carrie Thornton, Michael Morrison, Brittany Hamblin, and HarperCollins/It Books for believing in my vision and helping me see it through!